Strategic
Racquetball

Books By Steve Strandemo and Bill Bruns

The Racquetball Book.
Advanced Racquetball
Strategic Racquetball

Published by POCKET BOOKS

Strategic Racquetball

Steve Strandemo
with Bill Bruns

Photographs by Jack Miller

PUBLISHED BY POCKET BOOKS NEW YORK

Another *Original* publication of POCKET BOOKS

POCKET BOOKS, a division of Simon & Schuster, Inc.
1230 Avenue of the Americas, New York, N.Y. 10020

ISBN: 0-671-54745-3

First Pocket Books trade printing December, 1985

10 9 8 7 6 5 4 3 2 1

POCKET and colophon are registered trademarks
of Simon & Schuster, Inc.

Printed in the U.S.A.

Contents

Introduction

———————————●———————————

This is my third book about racquetball, and it reflects the insights and convictions I've gained about the sport since *Advanced Racquetball* was published in 1981. My earlier books provided the important fundamentals needed to build a successful all-around game. Now I want to expand that foundation with refinements, subtleties, and in-depth advice that will help make you a savvy competitor—on the challenge court at your club, in league competition, at local tournaments, or while enjoying an ongoing rivalry with your racquetball partner.

If you would love to upgrade your game a half-level to beat some players who are just nipping you now, then you *need* this book to help you recognize areas where you can improve and make competitive breakthroughs. Even if you've read my first two books, you'll find you learn much more about the game here—in terms of shot-selection strategy, technique improvement, and court coverage. I find I am continually gaining new knowledge myself, both as a player and as an instructor.

With this book, I'm confident I can help you become a better player by increasing your awareness of how the game ought to be played. As I travel around the country conducting clinics and teaching at my various camps, I find that virtually all players are held back by a lack of knowledge or a reliance on misinformation in one particular area or another. Some club players are frustrated because they have reached a playing plateau and they can't seem to bust through to the next level; they don't understand *why* they have a limiting style of play. Others assume that they have a correct and complete grasp of the game, and that a few simple adjustments will solve their current problems and make them much better players, while in reality they have stroking technique errors, some severe flaws in their shot-making strategy, and subtle mispositions in court coverage that keep them from maxing their potential. Even players at the open level are sometimes unprepared for my suggestion that their particular playing style will limit the progress they can make, and that important corrections are necessary.

So no matter how long you've been playing the game, try to put this book to work on your behalf—with an open mind. You may be pretty confident about your game and comfortable with your playing style, but if I can get you to evaluate it objectively against the concepts I'll stress in the pages ahead, you may realize that it has loopholes and voids that leave you open to defeat by certain opponents.

It's important to remember that the techniques and strategies I stress in this book are not far-out concepts that I have perceived in some think tank. Everything I teach is based upon my own playing experience and confirmed by my ongoing evaluation of top amateur and pro players in slow-motion videotape action. I've actually watched many five-hit rallies 40 to 50 times so I can totally understand what happens—and why it is happening—from shot to shot. Thus, my approach is a composite of all the methods that continually win racquetball matches, day in and day out, year after year. The type of racquetball game I want you to understand and *strive* to emulate has been distilled from years of collective experience and stripped of common misconceptions.

You may be thinking, "Steve's talking about serve-and-shoot racquetball and I don't have the power or the strokes or the inclination to play like that." That's not the case, though. I'll agree, the pros are flashy and power oriented, but don't be misled; when the game they are playing is slowed down on video and analyzed, several myths are dispelled and consistent patterns of play become clear and understandable—logical enough for any player to follow.

I'm not trying to present a revolutionary way of playing the game, although this realistic approach may challenge your own ingrained thought processes and playing style. I'm simply providing solid, basic information—the most correct, direct path to the improvement you are seeking. Once you understand and accept these basic concepts, we'll be on the same wavelength and we can go to work on the physical skills. If you fail to accept my major themes (for example, playing off leftup shots, shooting to an enlarged low zone, serving low-drives good or short, covering from a slightly deeper position, etc.), then your thinking process is going to be bucking the racquetball system. You may win a lot of matches as a result of your specific skills and athletic talents, but eventually you will come up against players who will exploit you unmercifully, and you will never reach your potential.

If you use this book to your advantage by making necessary changes in your stroking technique, improvements in your various shots, changes in your positioning, and adjustments in your shot-making strategy, you're bound to reach a higher playing level. One reason is that most of your peers reach a certain level of competence and then stagnate. They have some favorite shots and a particular playing style, but they stay with that game forever, and they never improve enough to advance beyond that point. Many players, in fact, seem to accept the plateau they're on, either unwilling to spend time practicing and improving, or unaware of just how much they could improve if they had a better understanding of the game—if they simply knew how all the bits and pieces come together and blend into a logical system. This is true at every level of the game. Or, they've resigned themselves to a belief that there's not a whole lot more they can learn about racquetball. It's as if they think that everyone has his or her own special way of playing and there is no standard to follow—but there *is* a standard, accepted way.

One of my basic goals is to help you develop an adjustable, diversified game that you can rely on in a competitive environment. Building this balanced game starts with an understanding that racquetball is logically broken down into two patterns: offensive (what I call "low zone") and defensive (or "high zone"). Solid racquetball players continually flow back and forth between these two areas in rallies, games, and matches. They have the shots to play the game low and hard as well as high and soft. They can rip the ball, but can also feather it up to the ceiling with good control. They can cut the ball off in center-court when it's appropriate, or pop what appears to be a low-drive ace accurately back to the ceiling.

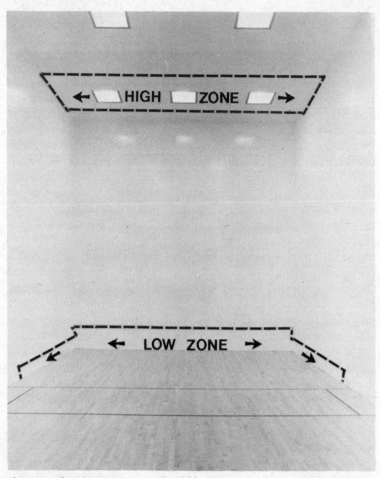

These are the target areas you should be aiming for on your offensive (low) and defensive (high) shots.

Only by having the ability to go low *and* high can you effectively cope with a variety of opponents. Yet, sad to say, most racquetball players have just one particular playing style. They have a favorite way of playing and they rarely deviate from certain predictable patterns. For example, a player may have an excellent low-drive serve and effective hard "Z's," but has never hit a high-lob "Z" serve in his life. Or, his shot selection is severely limited; he drives everything cross-court (only occasionally going down the line)

This offensive player is cutting the ball off in center-court, ripping low, and trying to score.

Here the receiver is flicking the ball to the ceiling off a near ace serve.

and fails to pinch many balls. This allows his opponents to lay back safely in a deeper coverage position, which in turn makes it more difficult for this player to execute effective passing shots. A third example is the person who prefers, whenever possible, to let every ball come off the back wall rather than seize those numerous opportunities to cut the ball off in center-court and score some relatively easy points. This prevalence of a one-dimensional game, where player X has just one system and sticks with it whatever may come, is an important reason why I feel tournament competition is a rewarding way to broaden your playing style.

A tournament forces you to play a cross-section of opponents with different strengths, weaknesses, and playing styles (providing, of course, that you survive the first round). You cannot dictate the type of opponent you play, and you must adjust in two key ways: first, by hitting shots you may not normally use under pressure, and second, by covering shots you may rarely see among your regular playing partners. Putting your game on the line like this is a challenging learning experience that forces you to come to grips with your strengths and weaknesses, and makes clear the areas where you need improvement.

I'm often amazed, for example, by the incompleteness of good players who have raised their game to a very respectable level in their own area, but who actually have serious voids that a smart player can easily exploit, especially in tournament competition where winning is the bottom-line concern. I once worked with two strong B players from Florida who had never hit a high-lob "Z" serve, or even returned one. They had played in a tight circle of friends back home and none of them had this serve in their repertoire. Had one of these two men entered a tournament in their home city, he would have been quite vulnerable to a well-rounded competitor; once the better player served a high-lob "Z" and realized he was facing a player who didn't know how to defend against it, he may not have used another type of serve the whole match.

So I think it's a great idea to stretch your game and test your various skills under pressure by entering tournaments or joining a league. I also encourage you to use videotaping as an unequaled method to study your game and to really understand how racquetball is played.

Don't pass up a chance to be videotaped; it will be an invaluable experience if you have an open mind.

I've used videotape analysis to improve my own game since the mid-1970s, and now it's an integral part of my instruction method. Playing the game at the pro level has been extremely important, but I wouldn't feel comfortable about analyzing racquetball and writing books about the sport if I hadn't spent years studying videotapes of the pros as well as club players. That gave me confidence in my judgments about technique, shot-making, and coverage, for I realized that only by studying videotape—watching one shot and one rally over and over again—could I fully understand the game. You can see the general plan by watching in person, but the action simply goes too fast to analyze accurately with the naked eye. Slow-motion videotape analysis is a necessity to isolate and study the important subtleties of your game.

With video cameras and recorders increasingly affordable and available, I recommend that you have a friend videotape one of your matches so that you can evaluate your game against the concepts and techniques stressed in this book. Watching yourself on video for the first time can be a little jarring, but after a few minutes you should be looking at yourself as just another racquetball player, and start studying yourself to see if all the parts of your game are working correctly. If they're not, it's time to re-program a little bit.

Your ego may get knocked back a little as you see your short-comings on video, but if you're objective about the evidence, this experience can help you make real progress. You may quickly realize, for example, that your non-hitting hand is touching the racquet every time you go to set up on the forehand, and that this is costing you valuable reaction time. Or you may find yourself saying, "I'm covering from the wrong position—way too far for-ward. No wonder I can't score from center-court." By studying yourself like this, as well as studying your opponent, you will see your tendencies and also how another person is trying to play you—what shots he is using to score points, and where he is positioned in covering your scoring attempts.

Perhaps the greatest value of videotaping is that it gives you an overview of the game in its entirety that you can never get while on the court, or while watching from the gallery. These insights are especially vital for enhancing your understanding of position-ing and strategy. For example, using slow-motion replays, you can see the exact moment when you were caught out of position, and why your opponent had an open alley to hit his winning pass. Video shows you the logistics of ceiling-ball rallies and can help you study the relative effectiveness of your relocation after serv-ing. In fact, you can watch a four-hit rally 10 or 15 times as you analyze first your serving motion, then the returner, then the movement of both players—body positions, anticipation, shot selection, and execution—and finally, coverage.

My intent in this book is to have a good, nitty-gritty con-versation about how racquetball *should* be played and what you can do to adjust your own playing style to conform to these basics. Without a proper understanding of solid play, too many elements of your game are left to chance, and you'll have ups and downs in your game so you'll be good one day, weak the next. I find that when people have this understanding about racquetball, they also have greater patience and work harder at incorporating new ideas and concepts into their game.

So ask yourself, "Have I thought the game out properly?" If you haven't studied the game, your incomplete knowledge can be a limiting factor in your improvement. If you feel your game is in a rut and you can't understand why you're not improving, it could be that you're simply thinking and hitting the same predictable way, without adding the offensive shots you may need, or employing a more offensive shot selection. We all know that racquetball improvement comes slowly, in fitful breakthroughs and gradual osmosis, but you can certainly hasten the process by studying your game with the help of this book and then applying your new information in well-focused practice sessions and matches at your club.

Some Common Racquetball Terms Used in This Book

ACTION ZONE: The back half of the court (a 20-by-20-foot area), where nearly all shots are contacted during a rally (after the serve).

AVOIDABLE HINDER: A hinder or interference, not necessarily intentional, which clearly hampers the continuance of a rally; results in a loss of serve or point.

CENTER-COURT: That approximate area between 22 and 32 feet from the front wall—and stretching to within about a foot of each side wall. This is the best strategic position on the court for low-zone play (leftup shots frequently funnel here) but is not the geographical center of the court.

FLY-KILL: To take the ball out of the air as it comes off the front wall.

HIGH ZONE: Refers to any shot up to the ceiling or side wall (*i.e.,* an around-the-wall ball) that is designed to keep or put your opponent on the defensive.

HITTING ALLEY: The lane the ball travels on its way to the front wall; ideally, where the ball should be hit to achieve the desired angle (*e.g.,* cross-court, down-the-line, or pinch).

HITTING ZONE: The vertical height of a player's hitting area (where he contacts the ball).

KILL-PASS: An offensive shot in which you try to kill the ball. If you do not succeed, the ball is hit at such an angle inside your low zone that it turns into an effective pass.

LOW ZONE: Your *effective* offensive target area for kill attempts, passes, and pinches along the side walls and into the front wall. A low-zone shot will take at least two bounces before the back wall.

LEFTUP SHOT: An offensive shot that fails as a kill in front of your opponent and kicks into the action zone as a hittable ball.

PLUM: A relatively easy offensive shot where you have plenty of time to set up.

PUT THE BALL DOWN: To hit an offensive shot that dies in front of your opponent (ideally, in the back of your mind, you're allowing a margin of error to hit a kill-pass).

RE-KILL: Taking a leftup shot and immediately trying to score with an effective low-zone shot.

SHOOT THE BALL: Hitting the offensive shot in a particular situation, rather than go to the ceiling.

WINNER: A shot that ends the point or wins the rally outright; any ball that bounces twice in any area of the court before your opponent can retrieve it.

1

A Shot-Making Philosophy

After working with a cross-section of players from all over the country the past ten years, I would venture that your overall playing style fits into one of these three categories:

1. You are too defensive, passing up numerous potential scoring opportunities because you think you should shoot the ball only when the conditions are perfect.

2. You are overly precise, thinking that you must aim for the bottom boards on practically every shot, even though this results in countless skips.

3. You have a reasonable understanding of the game and a melting pot of skills—accurate serves, kill-shot potential, and coverage ability—but inconsistency and key flaws keep you from making a breakthrough to the next higher playing level.

Wherever you might fit in, this chapter will help you start the process of building a more competitive playing style against a variety of opponents. My initial goal here is to get you into the flow of good racquetball by discussing the concepts that create a sensible shot-making strategy.

It's a fallacy to think you have to kill every ball consistently to be a successful racquetball player. You need to hit with enough power to end points off a good setup, and you should go for a kill shot when the shot is there, but kill shots seldom occur at the frequency you might hope and imagine. While this is certainly an offensive game, meant to be played aggressively, it is not a "total kill shot" game—even at the pro level. The pros dazzle the eye

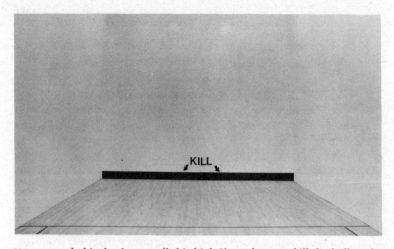

You can only hit the front wall this high if you hope to kill the ball, so be realistic: You don't have to kill every ball to be a good player.

The black area indicates "leftup" offensive shots that are not skipped or killed and that angle back into the action zone as hittable shots. As a defender, you should play off these shots.

with their speed, their kill-shot attempts, their gets, and a goodly number of rollouts, but the ball is left up much more than you think (a "leftup" shot is hit high enough into the front wall to allow for a return by the opponent). Everything happens so fast that spectators remember the spectacular winning shots, but not all the high and misangled shots before that winner (or skip!). That's an important reason why I prefer to rely on videotape analysis rather than the naked eye when I study the game.

Instead of thinking "perfect kill" on every shot, strive to hit as low into your "low zone" as possible—without skipping the ball. The "low zone" along the front wall and side walls is your *effec-*

When you are hitting offensively, think "low zone." Any shot hit into the black area will either be a kill or take two bounces before the back wall. You'll put incredible pressure on your opponent when you keep your shots in this area.

As you gain experience and skill, break your low zone into two parts: 1. the great area, where the ball will take two bounces before your opponent and go for a flat winner; and 2. the good area, where a properly angled ball will get by your opponent and not come off the back wall.

tive offensive target area for kill attempts, passes, and pinches. When you hit your low-zone area but fail to put the ball away, it will still bounce twice before reaching the back wall. This forces your opponent to cover the shot—knowing that he will lose the rally if it gets by him.

To find your low-zone range, drive a number of balls into the front wall from about 30 feet away, and have a friend mark where the ball hits (with colored stickers, for example), but only on shots that bounce twice before reaching the back wall. This determines the top of your front-wall target area—no higher than about 24 inches for most club players. The side wall area will be about 12 inches (or lower) for pinch shots, since you want the ball to die before the front service line or the opposite side wall.

If you've been playing with the attitude that you have to hit the ball below 4 inches to be offensive, or that you can only be offensive when you have an absolute "plum," then the low-zone concept should add an important dimension to your game. Knowing your actual low-zone target areas should actually free you to be *more* offensive in your thinking, as reflected by comments from my summer campers. Said one woman, with obvious relief, "I now realize that my front-wall target is two feet high, and not two inches." Another student added, "Before camp, when I went low zone, I was aiming as low as possible—bottom boards. One great shot and nineteen skips. Shooting the ball doesn't seem so scary now with my target area a lot higher."

When you're shooting, go for the kill—but if you miss, "error up" on the front wall and avoid the skip as often as possible. Many aspiring young players are convinced they must pound the ball hard and hit rollouts at every opportunity—"just like the pros"—but they continually skip the ball in, handing their opponents one gift after another. These players think that a high percentage of skips is just an accepted fact of life as they try to emulate the pros. What they fail to realize is that the pros know that when they fail to put the ball down (kill it), they can still apply relentless pressure with offensive shots that stay off the back wall and don't skip.

Juniors, for example, will get a good rally going and hit a lot of tough shots, but then skip in an unnecessary shot trying for the

This two-person drill will help you find the top of your low zone. It's critically important that every player find his or her own low-zone height. (Please note that the numbers here indicate where the ball will bounce.)

DON'T SKIP!

Aim for the black area but realize you can miss up to the dotted line (which is the top of your low zone) and still keep the ball off the back wall.

perfect winner. If they were to have this approach against the top players they think they are emulating, they would get drubbed. What they overlook is that experienced players have worked through the misconceptions of their early years; they still hit the ball hard but they also know the value of missing the kill in the right areas—*inside* their low-zone ranges. (I remember playing an eighteen-year-old hotshot who had just entered the pros. He shot everything when we played and skipped with such a frequency he practically handed me the match. But about four years later I saw this same player against a younger upstart, and he was now shooting the aggressive *percentage* shots. It's amazing what a few decisive whippings and some years of experience will do to a player's shot selection.)

So this should be your thinking process and a reasonable goal: aim as low as you can, but be satisfied with any shot inside your low-zone area, and happy when you pick up the kill. It's unrealistic to think—even when you have an absolute setup—that you're going to flat kill the ball, "bottom two inches," every time. But with additional experience, it's very reasonable to hit inside your low-zone area with power and control, applying pressure on your opponent with kill-passes and *slightly* leftup pinch shots. It's also inevitable that when you try to shoot like this while setting up, or on the run in a fast-paced game, that you're going to skip some balls in, but this should only occur infrequently.

Plenty of balls are put down, but what counts is your ability to capitalize on your opponent's leftup shots. Study videotapes of any tournament match in the country—at any level—and you'll be convinced that hitting too high on the front wall is inevitable for every player. Even in gift situations, the pros often leave the ball up because it takes precise accuracy to flat kill the ball, especially when you must hit while on the move or stretched out.

Knowing that leftup shots are inevitable—for both you *and* your opponent—is another factor that should help you become more aggressive in your shot selection. Instead of thinking, "If I can't kill it, I shouldn't shoot it," just hit the ball hard but safely into your low-zone area so that your opponent must hit again if you don't kill it. At least give him the option of making a mistake, for he'll miscue more times than you thought possible.

I once worked with an open player who was frustrated by the fact that as hard as he hit the ball, he had trouble scoring points against consistent opponents. I watched him play a quick match and the problem was obvious: he was going for the bottom board every time he shot—winding up with far too many skips—or opting for a ceiling-ball shot when he actually had a low-zone opportunity, if not a reasonable chance to kill the ball. When I talked to him about this he admitted, "I'm afraid to leave the shot up because I think my opponent is going to put the ball away. So I aim for the flat-out kill every time I shoot, and if I'm not confident about that, I go to the ceiling." After he studied videotape, however, he realized that his typical opponent failed to re-kill most of his leftup shots. Therefore he didn't have to hit the ball as low as possible in order to be effective within a low-zone type of rally.

So when you're shooting low, realize that, although you may be going for a winner, the odds are good that you will leave the ball up, but that your opponent will not cash in on his re-kill attempt—so you must be ready to move quickly and re-score. By keeping this sequence pattern in mind, you'll be mentally ready to shoot and you won't be surprised by misses that come right at you and could otherwise jam you up.

My shot-making rule of thumb is: if you think you can hit your low-zone area (i.e., keep the ball off the back wall), go for the offensive shot. Otherwise, go to the ceiling but be looking for the first low-zone opportunity. This basic advice puts the emphasis on taking all the reasonable scoring shots that come your way, while recognizing the importance of developing a ceiling-ball game (which I'll discuss in Chapter Three). By giving priority to this shot-making approach, rather than relying on defensive skills and an opponent's skips, you take more control of your destiny on the court.

For example, if the opening is there and you shoot and make it, great. If you shoot and leave the ball up, your opponent has a chance to win the rally, but he could just as easily leave *his* shot up—thus giving you twice as many scoring opportunities in this little three-hit sequence. This approach works because players are inefficient shot-makers at every level.

On the other hand, when your shot-making instincts are too defensive (if, for example, you are needlessly going to the ceiling), you're passing up too many offensive chances. And whenever your opponent has a shot, you'll be thinking, "I hope he skips it in," because that's about the only way you can score points.

This defensive approach may work in a tournament situation against the shooter who skips one shot after another; just keep the ball in play and he'll hand you the match. "Not very smart," you tell yourself, "but I'll take the victory and move on." Yet in the very next round, you may face an opponent who knows how to hit the front wall and forces you to earn every point. If you then can't blend offensive skills with your defensive abilities, plan on getting blown out.

Making the Transition to a Low-Zone Game

Now that I've highlighted the reasons why I feel a low-zone philosophy makes sense in today's game, the challenge is to make the necessary adjustments in your style of play.

If, for example, your goal is to open up and play the game more offensively, you must be able to shoot the ball when the chance arises (a skill that will be addressed in later chapters), and you must acquire an aggressive attitude. If you can hit a particular shot into your low zone, but your mind is not thinking offensively, then your body is not going to respond in time. But once you can train your mind to be offensive whenever there's an opportunity, I guarantee that your body will react automatically.

At first, you may have to exaggerate your offensive philosophy as you play in order to break ingrained defensive patterns and reactions. Work on your low-zone shots as you make this transition and force yourself to hit these shots at every reasonable opportunity when you play your practice matches—even if it means losing games you might normally win. (Also be sure the final outcome is unimportant to your opponent, especially if you have a higher ranking at the club. Otherwise, as you're trying to improve your shots while incorporating a new shot-making philosophy, he's likely to score an easy victory, and before you can get outside the court, the final score will fly down the corridor. That can be a little discouraging psychologically if you take pride in your racquetball game.)

Actually, when you open up your shot-making philosophy and vow to be more aggressive when you go into a match, you can

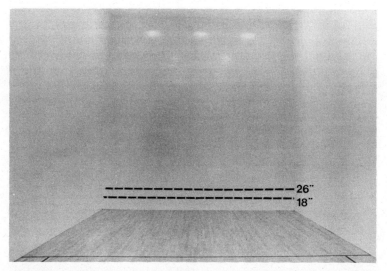

If you rip the ball, 18 inches is as high as you can hit on the front wall and still keep your shots from coming off the back wall. Another good player who doesn't rip quite as hard can hit up to 26 inches high.

sometimes upgrade your game immediately. Your greater emphasis on going low zone and the immediate pressure this applies to your opponent's defensive skills can often turn a stagnant game into a progressive one.

Meanwhile, on a practice court especially, you should strive to get comfortable hitting into your low-zone range on the front and side walls. To help visualize this area, put tape on the walls at the highest points for successful kill-passing shots and pinches, and then see just how many shots you can hit below the tape. This will help get your low-zone areas fixed in your mind and let you know exactly what has to be done to hit offensively. Really focus on that low-zone range as you hit, so that you'll begin to react instinctively in competitive situations.

If you're making the transition from a passing, retrieving type of game where you never really worried about hitting "low zone," you may have to skip a lot of shots in practice matches as you grow accustomed to scoring. Also remind yourself to "shoot down," for there's a persistence required here to keep the ball low as you strive to be offensive.

2

Low-Zone Racquetball

•

Whether a rally starts with an aggressive serve or a lob, the point is almost always decided by a low-zone shot that is either skipped, killed, or goes by the opponent for a winner. So let's now talk about the specific situations that you'll face continually in low-zone scoring rallies. I want to get you into the flow of good racquetball, where the hitting and coverage patterns are logical and you try to capitalize on the reasonable opportunities within this style of play.

Be Creative in Your Low-Zone Area

Remember my cardinal rule of shooting: you're looking for every opportunity to win the rally immediately, but instead of worrying that you have to kill the ball, just go for the lowest shot you're capable of hitting within your low-zone range. Even if you fail to hit an outright winner, hitting one of your targets inside this area will result in shots that put tremendous pressure on your opponent to cover. And if you hit low but miss your exact target, you're also going to score points with unplanned shots; you may be hitting on the run, for example, trying to go down the line, but your shot turns into a perfect side-wall pinch. You'll never get the benefit of errors like this when you hit *above* your low-zone.

Ideally, you'll try to be creative within your scoring range by mixing up your shots and learning to use the entire low-zone area to put offensive pressure on your opponent. Strive to hit the obvious open lane when he's out of position, but also learn to angle the ball away from him during a tight center-court exchange.

Another key point: *hit the ball hard to win points and end rallies*—don't rely on junk shots to "fool" your opponent. If you leave a junk shot up high, it will come off the front wall slow and tantalizing, as if to tell your opponent, "Here it is on a tee—now you can hit it." I prefer an attitude where you hit the ball with pace and conclude, "If I miss it, my opponent had better get his tail in gear, because he doesn't have much reaction time."

Of course, taking the pace off a hard shot, as opposed to hitting junk, is a legitimate goal if you can learn to control the ball—like a fast-ball pitcher who catches the hitter off-guard with a great change-up. Skilled players try to take the pace off the ball in a center-court rally (or in regular rallies when the opponent is lagging especially deep) by sliding or pinching the ball away from their opponent.

The Three-Hit Sequence

I think racquetball makes greater sense—and I know it's excellent mental strategy—when you visualize a three-shot sequence every time you go to hit the ball low. Basically, you're going for a winner, but you're expecting your shot to be leftup, so you're ready to cover your opponent's low-zone return. By always expecting the ball to come back low and hard, you're not surprised when your opponent gets to a shot you thought was a winner and makes a great retrieving return. Many players are caught flat-footed in this situation and are not ready to rehit—low zone—if the shot is there; instead they must weakly flick the ball back to the front wall or up to the ceiling. But when you remind yourself that even when you hit an excellent low shot the rally is not automatically over, you won't be jammed or caught sleeping by a quick-reaction return shot into center-court.

This is a logical way for me to think, since I know—after studying many matches on video—that I'm going to leave up many more shots than I kill. My opponent also knows how to play, so if my scoring attempt kicks into an area where he can try to re-kill, he's ready, and I'll then be anticipating *his* leftup shot as he tries to put the ball away. This type of thinking and shot-making should occur whenever the ball is hit offensively in a low-zone rally.

The Kill-Pass Theory

When you have a good setup in the center-court area and you decide not to pinch, your smartest shot is a kill-pass attempt. You go for the kill, but you think "low zone," either down-the-line or cross-court. If you miss the kill but hit the correct angle—you're just a little too high—the result is still a perfect pass. Your opponent must either try to cut the ball off—a difficult, fast-reaction play in center-court—or let it go. Either way, you've increased your offensive percentages by avoiding the temptation to hit such a perfect kill that you skip the ball in, rather than force your opponent to hit again. Remember what I stressed in Chapter One: it's totally unrealistic to think you have to try to kill every ball to be a good racquetball player. The kill target is simply too low and small an area for players to hit into all the time, so give yourself a margin of error by going for the kill-pass when the opportunity is there.

Passing Shots

My goal here is to motivate you to spend time on an empty court trying to groove your hitting angles into the front wall. Only a matter of inches separates an effective cross-court pass—one that may hit low and bounce on the floor between the side wall and your opponent—from a pass that rebounds off the back wall for a setup. The same concern for accuracy is required on a down-the-line pass, where you should bring the ball back inside the doubles box (an alley about 18 inches wide).

When you're going down-the-line and your opponent is out of

The kill-pass is a smart player's reasonable approach to down-the-line and cross-court scoring. You're shooting to put the ball down, but if you leave it up a little too high, it turns into a good pass. (The X on the court indicates an opponent.)

position, don't try to shave your pass so close to the side wall—
going for the perfect pass—that you risk catching the wall and
giving your opponent a reprieve as the ball kicks back to the
middle. This is also a common error among many players who
have a shaky grasp of geometry angles. The key here is to hit your
pass attempt closer to the middle and let it slide to the side wall as
it nears the back corner.

On the cross-court pass, when you're trying to get the ball into
the back corner, most players err by hitting the ball too close into
the front left corner. They seem to think the ball will somehow
travel straight down the side wall, but geometry won't allow this.
Instead, you must simply learn to hit balls that make more or less
straight-in angles to the front wall and then sense, through experience, how to let the ball work its way to the back corners.

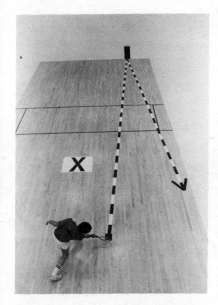 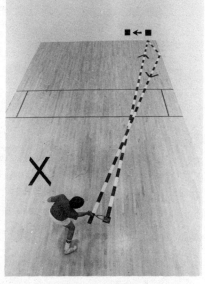

When you attempt to kill-pass down the right wall, you want the shot to travel near the doubles box lane. This keeps the ball off the side wall and gets it by your opponent.

When you have your opponent pushed to the side (indicated by the X), you may find you tend to hit your kill-pass too near the side wall, as shown here. Adjust your target closer to the middle and this will keep the ball from kicking back to center court.

Pinch Shots

If you want to know just how good your pinches are, get on an empty court and see where the ball takes its second bounce after you've hit low and tight into a front corner. If that second bounce

When you're diversifying your offensive attack, your pinches will take two bounces before either the front service line or opposite side wall, and will give you an uncontested winner.

is inside of 15 feet (the front service line), you'll have an uncontested winner against nearly any player. If your opponent is actually able to contest that shot, then he's either covering too far forward and is vulnerable to the wide-angle pass (pp. 159–60), or you may be too predictable in your shot selection.

When the ball carries a bit deeper, say to about 18 or 19 feet, then an opponent in center-court might reach it with good forward movement (i.e., one good stretching step). However, if your opponent doesn't cover well forward and positions himself at about 26 or 27 feet, then a pinch attempt that takes its second bounce at 20 feet could still be an uncontested winner. You'll have to see how effectively your opponent covers your pinches, and react accordingly.

When practicing, notice how side-wall pinching angles get closer to the front corner as you move toward the center of the court to hit. If you have a sound swing, you might also want to experiment with overspin on the shot to keep it down as it comes off the front wall.

THE REVERSE PINCH

Reverse pinching is great—*if* you can put the ball down in front of the short line. This ability gives you an offensive variable that will draw some ooh's and aah's from the gallery. In many situations, the reverse pinch is an appropriate and valuable shot, and needs to be in your repertoire. Unfortunately, players often get carried away, using it instead of a higher percentage shot.

Like any pinch, when you leave this shot up, the ball inevitably kicks into center-court for an easy kill attempt. More importantly, you've very likely overlooked a higher-percentage shot—the kill-pass attempt. When you're in center-court and there's an open lane down the right or left wall (see photos), why try to reverse pinch when the passing option is so much safer and still highly effective? Either you kill the ball straight in or it turns into an irretrievable pass down the wall (providing you hit inside your low zone).

If you can hit straight in, pinch, and go cross-court—confidently and effectively—there will be times when you can choose

If you're 5 feet off the side wall and 30 feet from the front wall, you can contact the side wall anywhere from zero to 15 feet to get a good pinch scoring angle.

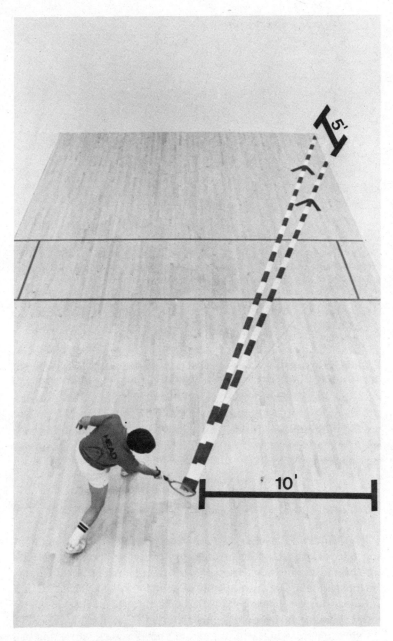

If you're 10 feet off the side wall and 30 feet from the front wall, you must move your side-wall contact to the 0- to 5-foot range.

If you reverse pinch and make the shot (as indicated here), that's great, but any leftup shots will kick into center-court for a setup for your opponent.

to mix in the reverse pinch. But until you have command of these basic shots, don't bank on the reverse pinch to win key points or key matches.

Pinching and Passing Strategy

You should build your game around pinches and complementing kill-passing shots because they force your opponent to play you "honest" in his coverage. Instead of camping in certain areas, he must standardize his position and can't afford to "cheat" either up, back, or to a particular side. This in turn makes him more vulnerable to your good offensive shots.

For example, when your opponent knows you can drive the ball cross-court or go down the line, he is forced to cover from pretty

When you have your opponent out of position like this, you should avoid gambling with a reverse pinch. The smart player will often hit a kill-pass down the right wall in this situation.

much the middle of the court, since he must respect both sides. But if he finds he can cheat 2, 3, or 4 feet into a preferred and predictable hitting lane, this shrinks your effective passing angle and you'll find it hard to score points.

Meanwhile, your ability to mix in pinches will also force your opponent to respect the front part of the court. If you seldom pinch the ball, he will lag back, especially when your kill attempts and passes rarely bounce twice inside of 15 or 20 feet.

Mixed and matched, the pinch and the pass complement each other in a well-rounded, diversified attack. Then what counts is your ability to be a creative *and* sensible shot-maker. Don't out-trick yourself by going for a reverse pinch when a straight-in shot will do the job, and avoid falling into predictable hitting patterns.

For example, many club players have been told, "When your opponent is ahead of you, pass him, and when he's behind you, pinch it." That may be logical in theory, but it's too rigid a formula for good racquetball play. Many times, you'll be in front of your opponent but realize that you have an open passing lane that is easier to hit than your pinch target. Equally important, if your opponent knows you're going to try to pass him every time he's ahead of you, then he'll start dropping back as you go to hit—4 or 5 feet perhaps—and it's now virtually impossible to pass somebody who's already standing in deep court.

In a similar sense, as you advance in this game, don't be overly concerned about hitting to your opponent's "weaker" side. Even if he has a great forehand and a punch backhand, he has learned to become efficient with his particular technique (and may even score on a few backhands). So simply strive to hit the open areas away from your opponent, on both sides. This forces him to hit while on the move or stretched out, greatly reducing his ability to score. Meanwhile, he has to play you straight up on defense.

(The quickest way to sense the "open" side is to remember, "Where did the ball just come from?" If it has good pace, try to hit your shot away from that area, since your opponent is still near there—he's not fast enough to move suddenly across the court to fool you.)

Two problems can arise when you persist in hitting to your opponent's backhand: first, you overlook numerous open lanes to his forehand side, and second, you allow him to anticipate to his backhand side and gain coverage time, while he also cuts down your hitting angle. Pretty soon he's going to be standing over there waiting to punch his pathetic backhand into the front left corner and cause you a ton of grief.

When you force your opponent to work both sides of the court, however, he cannot protect his vulnerable backhand nearly as well, and you can begin to pick him apart.

A Checklist: Offensive Play

☐ Do you know the height of your low zone?

☐ Have you determined your various front-wall target areas?

☐ Whenever there is a reasonable offensive shot, are you taking it into your low zone?

☐ Do you accept the fact that you need to think offensively (low zone) about any ball that enters your hitting zone from just above ankle height up to your waist? (Even between your waist and shoulders, an offensive shot may be dictated by the situation and your good strokes.)

☐ Are you driving the ball and pinching so you keep your opponent honest in his coverage?

☐ Are you hitting the open lanes when your opponent is out of position?

☐ Are you thinking "kill-pass" instead of simply going for flat-out kills every time you have a setup?

☐ Do you understand the correct passing angles, especially when your opponent plays too far forward in his coverage?

☐ Are you working on the shots in practice that enable you to play offensively?

Center-Court Skills

One of the guidelines I use to judge a particular player is how effectively he or she can play in center-court—that area from just behind the back service line (20 feet) to about 30–32 feet. I'm not necessarily impressed by the person who can set up off the back wall and shoot with relatively good velocity and accuracy (though obviously this is an important skill). But if this same player is also aggressive about cutting off shots that are coming through center-court, and he can put the ball down from various hitting positions, then he's a player to reckon with.

Center-court play is a major area that really separates players at every level. Here are some of the distinct advantages you gain by cutting the ball off at every reasonable opportunity, instead of simply letting it come off the back wall for what some players erroneously think is always a higher percentage shot.

Cutting the ball off can enable you to score a lot of easy points. You have your opponent slightly outpositioned from his previous shot, and here's a quick chance to volley a shot away from where he is now positioned. Rehit away from where the ball came from, because that's the area where your opponent is still closely positioned. Even if you leave the ball up, your opponent is—ideally—pushed to one side, must hit on the run, and will have difficulty killing the ball.

You maintain your center-court position, enabling you to take offensive advantage of that positioning. When you choose to move back and play the ball off the back wall, you allow your opponent to move into prime center-court coverage position. You'll have a relatively easy, straight-in offensive shot off the back wall, but fewer of these shots are killed than you think. The pressure is on you to execute, for if you leave the ball up, your opponent should be ready to capitalize on his center-court position. You gain more time to set up for a low-zone shot when you play the ball off the back wall, but the tradeoffs can get you in deep trouble.

You keep pressure on your opponent by denying him a reprieve for hitting slightly too high on the front wall. Instead of retreating to the back wall and allowing him a chance to reclaim center-court, you force him to respond quickly to your re-kill attempts and possibly hit off-balance or on the run.

You create a lot of psychological strain on your opponent. If he's setting up to hit and he knows you're just off to his side, ready to cover and rescore whatever he leaves up, then he's going to feel pressured to hit the ball really low and accurately—especially when you show that you can re-kill most of these shots reasonably low and hard. That's pressure racquetball. Conversely, if he knows you're getting up too close in center-court and just flicking most of his shots to the ceiling, then he's thinking, "Heck, this is like target practice."

You can hit a seemingly ordinary low-zone shot and still win the rally. Remember, the ball travels a lot faster than your opponent as he tries to cover your center-court shot, so this gives you a greater

Far too many players kick the ball up to the ceiling in center-court. You should, instead, be mentally prepared to be offensive against leftup shots in this area.

margin of error. You're forced to hit with less reaction time in center-court, but you're not taking the ball off the back wall and having to make a near-perfect shot. Just angle the ball away from your opponent and keep it in your low zone. For example, if he's pushed to the left and you cut the ball off, take it down the right side, or into the right corner, and you'll have a relatively easy point—without having to flat roll the ball. Very often, by just reacting offensively to your opponent's leftup shot, you catch him a little off-balance as well as out of position.

You're at less of a disadvantage when you leave the ball up. Since we fail to cash in as much as we expect when we have our setups, I'd rather hit my target area high from center-court rather than off the back wall. Even when I miss, I still have a positioning

The hitter, Terry Gilreath, has the defender pushed slightly off to her left side. The appropriate shot for her to make is a kill-pass down the right wall. She could also pinch into the right corner. Notice the hitter's open stance.

advantage. If my opponent does make the shot, he's probably off to one side or the other and must hit on the run, or will probably not have much time to set up on his shot. I am in the right position to take advantage of his weak recovery.

Execution

Deciding whether to cut the ball off or let it pass is a subjective feeling based upon your experience, how well you are hitting your shots in a particular match, and your opponent's positioning. Ideally, however, you should attack a ball coming through center-court that is *waist high* or below, and eventually you should be

Mike Yellen is adeptly cutting the ball off at about 27 feet, hitting at waist level with an open stance. This is good strategy because the defender is stuck behind him. Yellen's best offensive options are to pinch into the left corner or kill-pass cross-court.

All players should be thinking offensively on both the forehand and backhand against balls that can be contacted at any level up to waist level (area one in these photos). Hitting offensively above waist level will depend on the effectiveness of a player's strokes; players with great swings can pull the ball down from chest to shoulder level, but the majority of players should go to the ceiling against balls this high.

able to score fairly effectively with this shot. Waist level may sound way too high, but you must learn to accept this height if you want to play tough in center-court. As your skill increases and you catch your opponent way out of position, try to take a ball that is slightly higher than waist level and punch it down the wide-open passing lane. Shoulder-high balls are almost always taken off the back wall, for this is just too tough a shot to cut off and hit low-zone.

When cutting the ball off, there's rarely enough time to set up and get squared away, ready to step into the shot. The ball is traveling so fast that you'll be forced to hit from various body positions and footwork setups instead (see photos), and many times you'll be lucky just to get your racquet back and make good contact. So what counts is your ability to hit with good, quick upper-body strokes off both sides, and knowing how to do so from different stances—open to the front wall, off the back foot, on the run, stretched forward, and leaning back—with very little reaction time.

For example, I've noticed in studying Marty Hogan on videotape that he often doesn't move his feet when a ball comes quickly toward him; he just stands his ground, adjusts his upper body, and hits his forehand or backhand—not concerned about footwork. But on the very next shot, he'll be forced to use a cross-over step and stretch far to the side to cut off a potential scoring shot down the wall. That's the reality of good racquetball, not only among the pros, but on the serious club level. If your opponent shares your offensive thinking, be ready for a lot of good action in center-court. You might step into the ball and rip it low on one shot, but leave it up. He tries to rescore; now you must slide your body to the side and punch a shot into the corner. He covers; then you take a cross-over step and rip cross-court—and he's forced to flick the ball to the ceiling. This often happens when the ball is shot in low-zone racquetball and two players are trying to put their offensive shots down but can't kill it; each player fights to remain in center court, ready to pounce on any leftup shots. The players don't have much time to hit, but they know they must still try to hit low enough to keep the pressure on and the ball from coming off the back wall.

When you're shooting from center-court, hit the ball with some pop on it, but also learn to finesse it into the corners at different

Notice Marty Hogan's acceptable open stance as he hits off-balance and keeps his left arm in for balance. Since his opponent is pushed behind, Hogan attempts to put the ball down for a winner.

These photos are a reminder of how you must learn to hit from different body positions through the course of play, no matter where your feet are. Whether hitting a forehand or a backhand, you'll be forced to reach out in front of your striding leg or behind your back leg—and every position in between—while still being offensive.

speeds. Many situations will actually dictate that you slide a shot into the corner or push it away from your opponent, and if you can take a little power off these front-court scoring shots, the ball has a better chance of dying in front of your opponent. Remember, however, that "taking the pace off" doesn't mean dinking the ball, and that a leftup shot will come back to your opponent as a plum.

A final reminder: as you move to your center-court shot, accept the fact that your opponent is going to be near where the ball has come from, so as a basic shot-selection concept, *hit away from where the ball originated*. If the ball comes from the right side, try to hit down the left wall or pinch the front-left corner. And if the ball comes from deep left court, think about pinching into the right corner or hit down the right wall.

Acquiring a Center-Court Attitude

If you've been conditioned to play every possible ball off the back wall, then learning to hold your ground in center-court whenever possible will create some mental turmoil in the early going. Here are some points to help you make this transition to a more aggressive style of play:

Understand and accept the importance of cutting the ball off. As I'll stress throughout the book, every leftup shot coming through center-court is a potential offensive opportunity—the kind of shot you should be looking for to end a rally, not simply prolong it. If you hesitate too long, you lose a chance to score what is perhaps an easy point, and you must now try to earn the point from deeper in the court, off the back wall. I like to make the analogy to tennis, where a volleyer like Martina Navratilova hits a lot of easy winners at the net, while a player like Chris Evert Lloyd must earn almost every point from the baseline (or through an opponent's error). Actually, volleying in racquetball is even more accessible to the average player than in tennis, since you're already in or around the center-court area and you're not required to continually rush a net.

Remind yourself that it's natural to feel tentative and even a bit intimidated as you throw yourself into center-court play, since you're relying on different stroking demands and you're unsure of

If you have been overly defensive in your center-court approach, visualize this enlarged hitting area as you try to cut more shots off. Then, as you become more efficient and experienced, start moving the ball down toward your actual low zone.

just when you should cut the ball off. Here's where you must get on an empty court and hit shots to yourself in center-court that resemble these various leftup shots. Familiarize yourself with the angles and what it means to cut the ball off, then start worrying about accuracy. Through practice and match experience, you'll find your "cuttable area"—the height at which you can effectively score from center-court. Once you know you can pick out your options at your discretion, you'll be able to play aggressively.

Don't be inhibited by the fact that you rarely will have enough time to hit with "textbook" form. At first, you'll feel uncomfortable—even a bit inept—as you try to hit from varied positions with ad-libbed technique, but you can't let those feelings undermine your commitment to be offensive in center-court and to take the shot when it's there.

For example, if your opponent is hitting on the run and his miss kicks into center-court, don't automatically retreat to the back wall if the ball comes in a little high. Even if you're forced to hit while off-balance, you have your opponent out of position, and any good shot away from him—either a pinch or a passing shot— is going to be a winner.

A Checklist: Center-Court Play

☐ Are you ready to play off your opponent's leftup offensive shots?

☐ Are you far enough back in your coverage?

☐ Are you ready to hit low-zone, and rescore when the ball enters your reasonable center-court hitting area?

☐ Are you ready to hit from many different foot positions in center-court?

☐ Are you letting the ball come to you and hitting with your weight back when you're covering hard-hit passing shots that mis-angle to the middle of the court?

☐ Have you checked yourself to see that you're not touching your non-hitting hand to the racquet when preparing for a quick center-court shot?

☐ Are you hitting the obvious open lanes?

☐ Are you learning to shoot while on the run (a difficult but necessary part of the offense as you get into good play)?

☐ Do you understand that many times you may not score with your center-court shot, but by hitting your low-zone area, you'll keep pressure on your opponent and also hold a strong position in the rally?

Try to acquire an attitude in center-court that you're expecting the ball to come through this area and you're determined not to give up your position unless common sense dictates otherwise. One thought should be ingrained in your mind: be ready to score on every leftup shot. If you're forced to jam the ball up to the ceiling because you can't do anything else, that's fine. But if you're constantly forced up to the ceiling because you're not mentally ready to be offensive in center-court, then you have a serious problem holding your game back.

Once you recognize the virtues of trying to score from the center-court area whenever possible, the hard part begins—teaching your experienced body a new trick. Patience is needed here as you learn to hold your ground in an area where you have less time to react and hit, and your instinct is to let the ball pass so that you can play it off the back wall. In practice matches, really concentrate on your center-court skills—both mental and physical. Also, learn to do the 30-second drill (see Chapter Nine), so that you understand how to handle these leftup shots as they come to you in a match.

Give yourself two or three months to acquire some of these skills, motivated by the realization that you'll be much tougher to beat when they start falling into place. When you can combine good back-wall play with sound center-court skills, you have a scoring versatility that can beat your opponents many different ways in a low-zone rally. This is especially important on those days when your offensive serves are failing to earn a lot of points via weak returns and other areas of your game must take up the slack.

3

The High-Zone Game

⬤

Impressive as your low-zone skills might be, they can only take you so far in competitive racquetball today if you have an ineffective ceiling-ball game. Consider these reasons why the ceiling ball is so important and why you must become competent in high-zone play if you want to venture out against opponents with various playing styles:

1. The ceiling ball is the logical return off aggressive serves (low-drives and hard "Z's") that are too difficult to shoot.

2. It's the logical return off well-hit lob and high-lob "Z" serves that angle into you about shoulder-high.

3. It's the logical shot in a rally when you're pushed into an awkward hitting position—stretched out or on the run—and going low-zone is inappropriate.

4. Against a good opponent, if your lob serve dictates a ceiling return, you must be able to respond with an accurate ceiling shot of your own.

5. If your offensive game is not working in a particular match, you must be able to play more of a defensive game by changing to lob serves and therefore ceiling-ball rallies.

6. When you are competing against a capable opponent, and a ceiling-ball rally begins, you need to outlast your opponent with well-placed ceiling shots until he makes the first mistake and gives you a chance to hit low. Without a reliable ceiling shot off both sides, you will be forced to shoot when you should be defensive, giving your opponent continual leftup opportunities.

Ceiling-Ball Technique

I find as an instructor that most players lack a good ceiling-ball swing and rarely spend time trying to perfect this stroke.

On the forehand side, hitting your desired ceiling target with good touch is the important factor, so try to swing from an open stance with an easy ball-throwing motion. This should be an easy *directional* shot and definitely not a forceful effort. Many advanced players, at ball contact, come slightly across the ball and cut the shot. This takes pace off the ball and helps the shot come in good, or at least short of the back wall.

On the backhand, use the same stroking motion that you should be using when you hit the ball low—pulling all the way through with your shoulders and finishing with your stomach to the front wall. This shoulder motion is crucial, for if you try to punch the shot with just your arm (as so many players try to do), it is nearly impossible to have a consistent, accurate shot. Hit this shot from a closed-foot position when the ball is near your backhand side wall.

The Target Area

Use practice sessions to define and refine your target areas on the ceiling. Aim from about two to seven feet back from the front wall (depending on the ball speed), so that your shot will take its first bounce at around the front red line (15 feet), travel in a high arc, and strike about 2 feet up on the back wall. When properly hit like this, a ceiling ball will approach your opponent at chest-to-shoulder level. Since most players are not effective with an offensive shot from this height in deep court, a good ceiling ball usually dictates another ceiling ball, which is what you want.

If you err on a ceiling shot, at least hit the ceiling. Even if the shot comes in short, your opponent must still change the direction of the ball and his offensive attempt could easily go astray. Conversely, when you miss the ceiling and hit high on the front wall, your opponent gets an easy setup off the back wall, since the ball is already traveling in the desired direction. There's a huge difference in skill demanded in executing these two shots.

Notice the hitter's open stance on this forehand ceiling stroke, and his easy ball-throwing-type motion. Remember: It's not how hard you hit but *where* your shot contacts the ceiling that counts.

The backhand ceiling stroke is usually executed with a closed stance (especially when you are near the left wall). Notice how the racquet is set below the shoulder on the backswing and then comes up into the ball. Strive for the same good shoulder motion used to hit the ball offensively, but take pace off the shot.

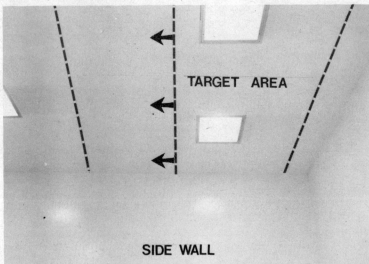

TARGET AREA

SIDE WALL

When going to the ceiling, aim for a target area approximately 2 to 7 feet from the front wall, as indicated by this photograph. If you think you're going to miss this target area, just be sure you hit the ceiling rather than high on the front wall to ensure that your ceiling shot will at least come in short.

Bring your ceiling balls in good or short. This forces your opponent to change the direction of the ball instead of giving him an easier shot off the back wall.

Simply hitting the ball too hard up into the ceiling will also bring the ball off the back wall. This problem often surfaces in tournament play, where players get so pumped up by the pressure that they tend to hit the ball harder than normal. If you recognize yourself here, especially as you play a first- or second-round match, then a good pre-tournament practice tip is to over-exaggerate your soft touch on ceiling shots, knowing that you are likely to hit naturally harder once play begins. Also, practice by yourself and see how long you can keep a ceiling-ball rally going by bringing the ball in good or short, while keeping it off the back wall.

Your Hitting Alley

Many players make the mistake of trying to hit a perfect ceiling ball down a narrow alley along the side wall, hoping that their opponent will be handcuffed by this "wallpaper" shot. Unfortunately, by perceiving a hitting alley only about 12 inches wide, these players have little or no margin of error with a slightly mis-angled shot to the left and the ball invariably catches the side wall and kicks off for a dead setup.

Instead of such an all-or-nothing strategy, try to visualize a hitting alley 4 to 5 feet wide, safely away from the side wall. By creating a bigger alley, you will give your opponent far fewer setups and you will still force him up to the ceiling. Remember, if you're bringing your ceiling shot in at the correct *depth,* regardless of *where* your opponent makes contact in deep court, he'll almost always go back to the ceiling with his shot. Also, if you reach top-level play, where the "splat" becomes an integral part of ceiling-ball rallies, keeping your ceiling shot 5 to 6 feet away from the side wall will negate your opponent's ability to splat the ball off a short ceiling. Top players find that trying to drive this shot (the short ceiling) down an open lane along the wall is much harder than splatting a similar shot from close to the wall.

Many players try to direct their ceiling shots down such a narrow alley (1) that they frequently catch the side wall. It's unreasonable to think anybody can be this accurate one shot after another.

A much more reasonable alley is this 5-foot lane (2). Strive to keep your ceiling balls in this wider alley, for even if the ball comes back 5 feet off the side wall, the vast majority of your opponents will have to kick that good ceiling ball back up if it has the correct depth.

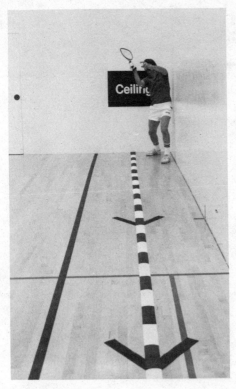

Even in good play, you will see a lot of forehand ceiling balls hit from the backhand corner; many players feel more comfortable and accurate with their forehands than they do with their backhands.

The Ceiling-Ball Rally

The ceiling-ball rally is an exchange of defensive shots, with each player looking for a slight miscue that allows him to take an offensive shot. This calls on you to have patience, coupled with an aggressive attitude, because virtually every ceiling-ball rally ends up in the low zone. Why? Well, after a succession of ceiling balls, one player will inevitably either (1) miscue long, short, or off the side wall—thus creating an offensive opportunity; or (2) mix in an overhead drive or kill attempt, which can force the action low.

This means you must be continually alert, ready for a high-zone rally to suddenly go low-zone. You can't afford to pass up an opportunity to attack slightly short ceiling balls, or to let your opponent catch you off-guard with an overhead that forces a weak return.

POSITIONING AFTER HITTING A CEILING BALL

After hitting to the ceiling, realize that your shot—whether good or not—is going to travel to deep court, so stay back until you read your opponent's intentions. Then either slide off to the side, ready to cover his ceiling shot, or move up to handle his low-zone attempt. When you hit a good ceiling shot, your opponent should be forced up to the ceiling while you wait for the ball to come back to you.

Too many players, however, think they should quickly move up to a center-court position after hitting a good ceiling shot, ready to cover their opponent's low-zone return. But when that return is another predictable ceiling ball, they must quickly retreat and will often get caught late, thus turning a routine shot into a difficult return. Many players are even forced to flick the ball to the ceiling, hitting over their shoulder as they run back, when they might have had an offensive shot had they simply stayed back to begin with. By routinely moving up to cover at around 25 to 27 feet and then retreating, these players also waste a lot of energy against the opponent with a sound ceiling-ball game.

The one exception to this advice comes when you play the rare opponent with overhead kill (not drive!) capabilities. When he proves that he can take even your good ceiling balls low into the front wall (several times in succession), you must cover about 3 feet farther forward than normal. Yet, as the match wears on, the chances are excellent that he will start leaving this shot up and bringing it right into center-court.

Once a ceiling-ball rally develops, you and your opponent should keep sliding off to the side, exchanging positions and alternating ceiling balls, until there's a mistake or one person deliberately takes the offensive. If you see that you've hit a weak ceiling, or one that is going to come off the back wall, you have plenty of time to move forward to cover your opponent's anticipated low-zone attempt.

STUDYING YOUR OPPONENT'S INTENTIONS

After hitting your ceiling ball and moving toward the middle of the court (between the side walls), you must constantly watch

The arrows show how opponents should rotate positions during a good ceiling-ball rally.

After hitting a good ceiling ball, some players make the mistake of moving too far forward to cover their opponent's next shot. This is illogical, for a good ceiling ball will dictate another ceiling ball, hit from deep court.

Once the defender sees his opponent going low-zone against a short ceiling ball, he should immediately move up to about 27 feet to cover his leftup shot.

READ: HIGH ZONE

HEAD

When you're in a ceiling-ball rally, watch your opponent and read from his body and racquet position if he is going high or low. When the racquet is laid back, he is going to the ceiling, and when the racquet is set high, he's going low-zone.

your opponent to see if he's going high or low. If you can't "read" this from his swing, you won't have the early anticipation needed to play this game right, especially when the action goes low-zone. Learning to read an opponent's swing and incorporate this into your game is easy to do with some conscientious practice.

STRATEGY WITHIN THE RALLY

Once you have a reliable ceiling shot up both sides of the court, you should strive to add a cross-court ceiling to your arsenal, both for variety and to use against a lefthander.

If, for example, you're overly predictable with your ceiling shots, always going up and down the left wall, certain opponents may try to rush up, take the ball on the rise, and jam it into the corner for a winner from about 15 feet. This can be intimidating if your opponent has the quickness and skill to execute this particular shot, but rest assured that he's giving you a strategic edge. You should retaliate by frequently going cross-court instead of

READ: LOW ZONE

simply up and down the line, for this will catch your opponent out of position when he moves up in anticipation. By mixing up your ceiling shots like this, you force him to stay back where he should be.

Learning to hit a cross-court ceiling to the deep right corner will also give many righthanders trouble, since most of them haven't practiced returning ceiling balls off that angle. Their obvious return shot is a cross-court ceiling to the backhand side (against righthanders), but they instinctively try to scrape the ball too tight into the back corner, and very often it catches the left wall and comes off as a setup.

Another way to diversify your high-zone game and show your opponent something different is to mix in an occasional around-the-wall ball—very judiciously. Let's say that you're wrapped up in a good ceiling-ball rally and you sense that you can catch your opponent off-guard with an ARWB, hitting with the same backhand ceiling motion but glancing the ball off the left wall. Your opponent is lagging deep alongside you, anticipating a ceiling shot, and he's therefore not able to move up quickly enough to cut the ball off in the air after it comes off the right wall, so it angles

Learn to diversify your high-zone attack by incorporating an around-the-wall ball into good ceiling-ball rallies. Notice how the hitter executes a subtle glancing shot into the side wall off the same motion he uses to hit a ceiling ball.

diagonally across the court toward the left wall. He is then forced to make racquet contact before or after the ball hits the left wall and—against a good ARWB—will probably take the ball back to the ceiling.

So what does all that gain you? Instead of trying to beat your opponent with the same basic ceiling-ball pattern, you force him to contact the ball at what may be an unfamiliar angle up to the ceiling and he may now err and give you an offensive shot. But don't expect flat winners off this shot against a good opponent. Also keep in mind that if you miss your ARWB target, you hand your opponent a setup.

HOW TO GET OUT OF A CEILING-BALL RALLY

Occasionally you will come across the painfully methodical opponent who has pinpoint control of his ceiling shots and the patience of a saint. If you refuse to play this type of game—out of impatience or perhaps because you have a weaker ceiling-ball game—here are some ways to get out of high-zone rallies:

If your opponent brings his ceiling ball in short, be ready to be offensive after the first bounce. Hitting from a closed stance near the side wall, you should learn to either splat the shot or kill-pass down the line or cross-court.

1. Be ready to shoot any ceiling ball that comes in slightly short or long.

2. Attack his slightly mis-hit ceiling shots with an overhead drive, aimed about 12 inches up on the front wall and directed away from your opponent so that he must contest the shot—knowing it will otherwise die in the backcourt without coming off the back wall. Unfortunately, this is a far more difficult shot to hit low than it appears, because most racquetball players are unaccustomed to hitting down from around shoulder level. But I've found that tennis players with a good serve in that sport will often have an excellent overhead drive in racquetball. (The accurate overhead is particularly effective against an opponent who has slow reactions, is tiring, or tends to lose his concentration during a long ceiling-ball rally, which makes him vulnerable to the unexpected offensive shot.)

3. If you're willing to take the risk, an overhead kill can certainly keep your opponent from grooving into a ceiling-ball ex-

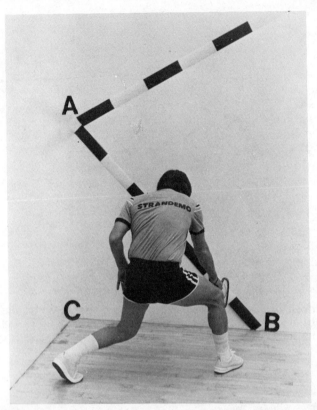

If your opponent hits a ceiling ball too hard and it comes off the back wall, make sure you hustle back far enough so that your feet are within the triangle formed by A, B, and C. This gets you behind the ball and ready to rip an offensive shot.

change. But that's asking a lot out of this high-angled pinch shot from deep court: it must strike the side wall about 6 inches high in order to die in front of your opponent. Hit higher than that, the ball is going to come into center-court as a "plum." Even if you have the skill to occasionally pull this shot off from such a high hitting angle, I still wouldn't rely on it at any crucial moment during a match. Simply save it as a surprise shot when your opponent is deep and anticipating a ceiling ball or an overhead drive, for this will give you some breathing room if you hit the shot too high. At least he must move a longer distance to reach the ball.

One pitfall to avoid when you're playing the ceiling-ball artist: in your aggressiveness to take the rally low-zone, make sure an offensive opening is there, or you will simply hand your opponent numerous putaway opportunities. I find that when players get lazy or impatient during a ceiling-ball rally, they tend to hit an overhead drive or a kill even when they lack command of either shot.

4. When a ceiling shot comes in short, and tight along the side wall (within 18 inches or so), many top players are learning to attack the ball with a hard, spectacular type of pinch shot called the "splat." This is not a spontaneous shot but one that is intended to nick the side wall several feet in front of the hitter and angle down into the front wall, where it can spin off as a pinch-kill.

The splat can give you an added offensive weapon, especially when your opponent is lagging back in his coverage expecting a kill-pass attempt, down the line or cross-court. But don't regard this specialized pinch as a mystique shot that is going to carry you to a higher plateau. Unless you really understand how and when to hit it, persistence with the shot will only take you lower, for it has a huge, inherent flaw: If the ball hits *slightly* too high on the front wall (higher than 12 to 18 inches for most players), it will invariably come off the opposite side wall and into center-court as a plum.

You shouldn't try to incorporate the splat into your game until you have a solid swing that generates good pace on the ball, and accurate kill-passing shots. I see a lot of strong players who overuse the splat because they have strong backhands and forehands and they can rip the ball when a ceiling ball or lob comes in short and close to the side wall. The splat looks great when they can roll it out, but they tend to forget all the times they leave it up. Many of these players become so dependent on the shot that they never develop the ability to go down the line with an equally effective and far safer shot.

4

The Serve

When you enter a competitive arena against opponents of varying playing styles (for example, in tournaments and league play), how many different serves can you accurately hit under pressure? Do you have only one trusted serve, or have you developed an arsenal that includes low drives, hard "Z's," high-lob "Z's," and lobs?

This chapter will try to help sharpen your serving skills, and perhaps broaden your repertoire so that you have (1) the flexibility to keep your opponent off-balance, unable to "cheat" in anticipation of a predictable serve, while (2) allowing you to exploit your opponent's particular weaknesses. Without this variety—and the confidence to hit the serve that is called for in a pressure situation—your potential success will be severely limited.

The Low-Drive Serve

Whatever your ability level, some nitty-gritty details may be limiting your low-drive effectiveness. Here are some key checkpoints:

1. Have you found your exact *hitting* range on the front wall? When players simply rely on "touch," they often fail to realize just how small their desired front-wall target is and how low they must consistently hit to keep their serves off the back wall. The best way to determine where you should aim, in relation to your power, is to have a friend place colored stickers on the front wall to

This photo shows the desired serving target for an open-level player who really rips a low-drive serve. His good area is between 11 to 13 inches on the front wall, and he contacts the ball in the service zone, approximately five inches off the floor.

Here's the target for a top B player who doesn't contact the ball quite as low as the open player and fails to hit as hard. His ball contact is 8 inches off the floor and his front-wall target is 16 to 18 inches high.

This player is getting ready to serve. When he uses a 2-step motion on low-drives and hard "Z's," the first step and the bounce occur at the same time.

indicate where the ball hits when you hit a low-drive serve that (1) lands between you and the side wall, and (2) bounces twice before the back wall. The area formed by these stickers is what you want to ingrain in your memory (adjusting your target laterally when you hit from different locations in the service zone).

2. Your ultimate goal is to keep this serve off the back wall, so if you're going to err by missing your ideal target area, do so *short.*

A low-drive needs velocity, but not at the expense of accuracy. If you can get the ball to land just past the service line (in that 20- to 25-foot range), nearly every serve will take 2 bounces before the back wall. But you should realize that when you are short on the first serve by hitting too low on the front wall, you still have a second serve that should force your opponent to the ceiling. Why risk losing your serving advantage by initially hitting a low-drive off the back wall for a setup?

This is the proper direction for a good low-drive serve. The ball must take its first bounce in the boxed area shown (between 20 and 25 feet) to keep from rebounding off the back wall. So serve it good or short.

The most common errors players make in serving low-drives are to hit the ball too far left or too high—or a combination of both.

To angle the ball into the back left corner, the server should hit the front wall about 2 feet to the left of where he makes contact in the service zone. Notice that this front-wall contact point is directly in front of the server's body.

3. In my mind, a two-step motion *toward the target* (a short preparatory step followed by a long stride forward) is still the most efficient way to maximize direction and then power into a shot.

Many players try to fool their opponents by stepping in one direction and hitting to another, but their accuracy doesn't allow them that luxury and they tend to misdirect the serve. Only after mastering a reliable serving motion should you try to learn to hit different serves off the same two-step motion, where you stride in a different direction than your actual target.

Also be sure here that you're not trying to hit the ball so hard that your momentum forces your trailing leg to come forward to provide balance. This back leg should act as your pivot leg for relocation, and if you let it swing around as you follow through, you'll be too far forward (by about 3 or 4 feet) to effectively relocate and handle a low-zone return. You want to stride forcefully into the serve, but keep your weight back.

When the right leg is positioned properly during a serve, as shown here, it can act as a good pivot leg for relocation.

Some players try to hit so hard that their right leg is thrown up in front of the 15-foot line. This leaves them too far forward to relocate and cover an opponent's immediate low-zone return.

4. Your actual hitting motion should incorporate the key elements of a sound forehand stroke as you strive to contact the ball as low as comfortably possible. Three common problems:

- Instead of taking the racquet back and then down through the ball with one continuous motion, some players set the racquet early, hesitate, and then come down. This allows the returner to easily sense the intended path of the serve.

- Many players are afraid to snap the serve straight in to the front wall, for fear of getting hit by the ball. As a result, they have a tendency to come across their body and pull the ball left of their desired target area, sending it rebounding off the left wall as a setup.

- Most players also have a tendency to hit too high into the front wall because they bounce the ball too high as they stride into the shot, or they fail to let the ball drop low enough before contact. They are hitting on too high a plane.

Photo 1 is a correct and fundamental starting position from which to serve either of the hard serves (a low-drive or a hard "Z"). Taking the racquet back within the serving motion, rather than setting the racquet early (as in photo 2), helps keep the receiver from reading your serving intentions.

This photo is taken from the ball's point of view as it comes off its ideal front-wall target and is heading for the blackened area on the court. When you realize how tiny this area is, you can appreciate how difficult it is to serve a good low-drive—and why, when you miss, it is far better to serve short.

This is a side-wall view of the arc taken by a good low-drive serve. To achieve this arc, you must make low ball contact and hit with a slight upward arc into the front wall.

5. Once you've determined your front-wall target area, try to bring the ball into this area on a slight *upward* arc. This enables you to hit the ball hard and still have it carry just past the short line on a low, skimming angle. (At contact, try to get the racquet low via good leg bend, but realize it's also quite acceptable to drop the racquet face to make lower contact.)

RELOCATION

Good relocation after the serve actually starts with your two-step motion into the ball. After hitting off your left foot (if you're a righthander), you want to be able to pivot quickly around on the trailing right foot and drive back with the left leg. Then use a couple of basketball-type shuffle steps to reach your initial coverage position at about 24 feet, near the middle of the court.

(If you're baffled as to why you're continually jammed or passed by an opponent's low-zone return, one reason could be that you're letting the trailing leg swing forward after serving. You can correct this problem by simply practicing the desired movements: Plant the front foot as you hit an imaginary serve, then pivot off the back foot and pull back with the front.)

Ideally, you should see where the ball is going as you take your pivot-back step; then begin to study your opponent's intentions up until the moment he contacts the ball. This will maximize your anticipation and coverage ability. If you simply take a quick peek at your opponent and then turn back to the front wall before he actually starts his swing, you'll have no idea if he's going low-zone or high-zone with the return.

When you see your opponent going to the ceiling, immediately retreat, since your next shot is going to be hit from somewhere in deep court and you want to be in an appropriate position to either shoot or go back up to the ceiling yourself. If you hesitate around the service zone too long, you will find yourself in a race with the ball and be forced to flick the ball back to the ceiling way too often.

If you see that you've hit a high or mis-angled serve, you can anticipate a low-zone return, so what counts is how well you can read your opponent's body motion in order to sense *where* he's trying to go with the shot. Equally important, as I stressed earlier in the book, is the fact that you want to be mentally and physically

The server should watch the path of his serve into the back corner as he pivots on his right foot.

Later in his relocation, the server is studying his opponent to see what is going to be hit.

Unfortunately, a lot of players are in this position when their opponent is hitting. They don't even know if the ball is going "high or low," and are unable to anticipate a down-the-line or cross-court return.

The server is peeking at his opponent, uncomfortable about turning to get a better view, and will thus be less effective at anticipating and covering a low-zone or high-zone return.

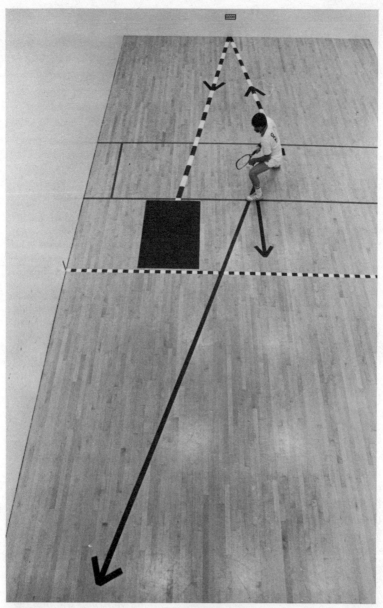

When the server relocates after hitting a low-drive serve, he tries to gauge what his opponent is going to do. If he reads his opponent going to the ceiling, he immediately hustles to deep back court. If he sees his opponent going low-zone, he works hard to locate at about 24 feet and to be ready to play off a leftup shot.

ready to cover his leftup shot aggressively. Instead of thinking you should relocate at about 20 feet when you know you've hit a lousy serve (in order to cover your opponent's kill attempt), remember the shortcomings of this strategy. You still can't reach a shot that dies inside 15 feet, and you will be easily handcuffed by many of the hard-hit shots that are left up. So, as a result, you're ineffective against most of your opponent's low-zone returns.

A final note about relocation. After serving your low-drive into either corner, the temptation is to shade (cheat) to that side as you relocate, in order to cover the down-the-line return. However, this opens up too much of the court for a cross-court pass by your opponent. Better to relocate directly back so you can react to a variety of returns from a more equidistant point.

The Hard "Z" Serve

Many players find that the hard "Z" is an untamed beast—a necessary ally with great potential, but difficult to harness under the pressure of competition. There's such a tiny margin of error hitting into the front wall that most hard "Z's" tend to come in short off the back wall, long off the back wall, or mis-angled down the middle of the court—all of which give your opponent a return he should shoot. Even a seemingly perfect "Z" can jump off the back wall at the last moment. Errant "Z's" also force you to give up vital coverage area as you relocate.

Still, you can't avoid hitting hard "Z's" in a competitive environment, for this serve complements the low-drive, putting pressure on the receiver and keeping him off-balance by presenting different hitting angles. When you can angle the ball correctly into the front corner, it will cut across the court and often force a weak or defensive return.

POSITIONING AND BALL CONTACT

If you want your "Z" to travel to the back left corner, here are two reasons why you should position yourself close to the left wall, versus the middle of the court, as you go to hit:

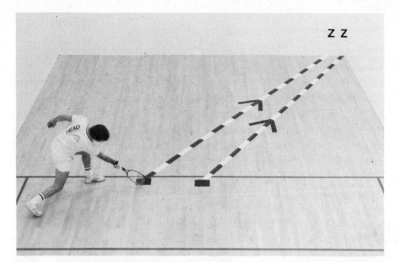

If you contact the ball directly in the middle of the service zone, you have to be consistently accurate to hit within inches of the right side wall and many mis-angled "Z's" will result. It is easier to hit correct "Z" angles from left of center.

If you are serving hard "Z's" from left of center and the receiver is cheating to the left side, keep him off-balance with a low-drive to the right corner (while occasionally mixing in a low-drive to the left corner). In this photo, the low-drive to the back left corner, created by hitting the box on the left, would cause a screen, but the server can usually avoid this by stepping to the right as he serves.

These are different target areas in the front corner that create different-angled "Z" serves: long, good, short, or mis-angled.

A properly angled hard "Z" serve will travel front wall, side wall, floor, side wall—and not come off the back wall. It's easier to hit the correct angle from left of center.

1. Geometrically, it's easier to hit the desired target area in the front right corner when you contact the ball 2 or 3 feet *left* of center than when you hit from the middle.

2. Using the same hitting motion, you can hit either the hard "Z" to the back left corner, or low-drives to both corners. Your ability to execute these three serves from the same position keeps your opponent from cheating to the left on your hard "Z."

You should hit the hard "Z" off the same motion as a low-drive and at the same height. Then strive to hit a target area that will create the desired path: front wall, side wall, floor, and opposite side wall—and not come off the back wall.

RELOCATION

Since many players are scared to serve a hard "Z" from the left side, fearing they will get ripped by the return, let's discuss what I feel is the most logical, efficient, and safest way to relocate after hitting into the front *right* corner.

After you serve, actually turn away from the ball—toward the left wall, or to the "outside"—and pick the ball up over your left shoulder before it bounces on the floor. You briefly lose sight of the ball as you turn, but this isn't important, since a good player will not try to make contact until this serve bounces on the floor. By turning to the left like this, you protect the front part of your body against an opponent who panics on the return, moves up, and wildly rips the ball cross-court. And by eliminating this fear, you can study your opponent's intentions as you relocate, right up until he contacts the ball.

Try to always relocate back into the middle of the court, then adjust your coverage position in relation to where the ball comes off the side wall or back wall. If you read from your opponent's swing that he's going high, quickly move back to cover his ceiling shot. And if he's going low, square off to the front wall and be ready to cover a leftup shot.

When your hard "Z" is short, long, or mis-angled, be ready to adjust your relocation position accordingly so that your opponent is free to hit low and straight to the front wall, as well as cross-court to the side of the court you're on. Many players are guilty of avoidable hinders on this serve because they refuse to move aside

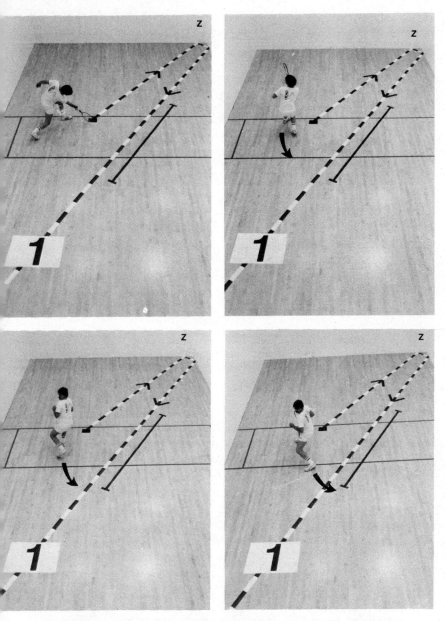

This sequence shows what I feel is the correct way to relocate on the hard "Z." The server does lose sight of the ball as it passes through the service box area (indicated by the solid black line), but that is unimportant because the receiver doesn't make contact until after the first bounce. Notice how the server immediately picks up view of the ball over his left shoulder as he turns back.

In good play, the receiver doesn't attempt to return a hard "Z" until after it has bounced on the floor. Also, through knowledge and experience, the receiver can start reading the serve's effectiveness by the time it reaches the service-zone area.

This is the other relocation option after hitting a hard "Z," and it clearly leaves the server in a precarious position. If he is a little slow in his turn and the receiver panics and hits an errant cross-court return, it could be "lights out" for the server.

This mis-angled short "Z" hits a little tight to the right side wall and often a little low on the front wall, and thus caroms directly to where the receiver is positioned.

The long "Z" takes the correct ball path, but is hit slightly too close to the side wall or too high on the front wall and will kick off the back wall. Notice how the ball rebounds to the receiver as a relatively easy offensive opportunity.

This serve hit too far away from the right wall and therefore takes an incorrect angle: front wall, side wall, floor, and then either off the back wall or a side wall for a setup.

as the ball travels from left to right off the side wall in the backcourt. Or, they turn back to the front wall too early, thinking they need to protect themselves, and they fail to adjust to where the ball eventually travels.

HITTING TO THE BACK RIGHT CORNER

Spend time practicing the hard "Z" that carries into the back right corner, not only for when you want to attack a lefthander's backhand, but to complement your low-drive to the left corner. For example, if you've burned your opponent in the left corner several times, and he's leaning in that direction, then off the same serving motion you can snap a hard "Z" into the back right corner. Before he can adjust, the ball will get tight into that corner and very likely generate a weak return.

Two hard serves hit off the identical motion are a low-drive to the left corner and a hard "Z" to the right corner. Mix these in with discretion to keep the receiver off-balance.

In serving hard "Z's" to the back right corner, relocation entails simply sliding back to the middle. No turn is necessary because your body angle in relocation is the same as when you contacted the ball. You lose sight of the ball through the service box, but this is insignificant.

When you intend to hit this particular serve, you can start near the middle of the court, providing you toss the ball to the right of center and make racquet contact to that side. This creates a nice hitting angle into the front left corner and can also be a little deceiving to your opponent, who might be anticipating a low-drive.

In relocating, track the ball over your right shoulder as you slide straight back in the middle of the court and watch your opponent. You don't have to work on a relocation turn because after you complete your serving motion you're positioned in the same body alignment that you desire, behind the service box.

The "Crack" Serve

In my opinion, this is too often a "feast or famine"–type shot in which you try to land a low-drive serve just beyond the short line and close to the junction of the floor and the side wall, hoping for an ace. The time spent on this serve could be far more profitably invested in a solid low-drive serve that you can rely on under pressure.

The "Jam" Serve

When used judiciously, this serve can catch your opponent napping and yield a weak return—but don't depend on it. For example, if he's conditioned to your regular low-drive serves, he may be caught off-guard when you angle the ball hard off the side wall and it either jams into his body or caroms around behind him toward the opposite side wall. *However,* if you hit this serve too high and at the wrong angle, you hand the returner an easy setup. Even an accurate jam serve can be effectively handled by a good player when he sees it coming.

Here's my thinking. When I hit a low-drive, I'm aiming low so that the serve is either good (usually forcing a weak return or a ceiling-ball return) or short. Either way, I don't automatically lose the serve. On a jam serve, though, I might win the point right away, but I can lose it just as easily if I miss my target. I would rather play the percentages.

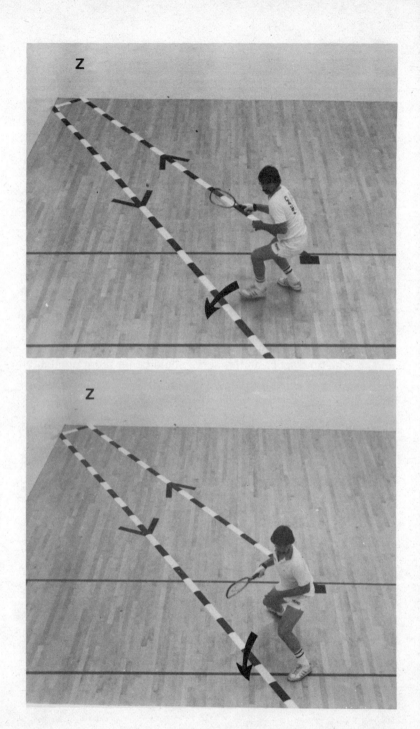

Even on the "Z" serve, some players make the mistake of letting the right leg come too far forward, as shown here. Keep this leg back so you can relocate efficiently.

This is a dangerous inside relocation turn, for at one point the front part of the server's body is opened to the receiver. You may play your whole life turning this way and never get hit, but just one errant cross-court return could cause a severe eye or body injury.

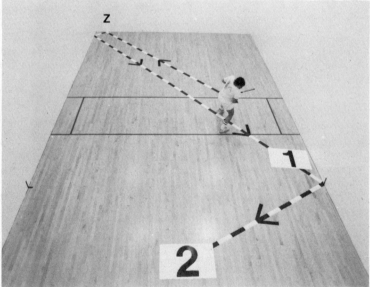

These photos illustrate the common problem of standing too far to the right when hitting a hard "Z" into the back right corner. If the "Z" is short and kicks in behind the server, he doesn't know where to go and oftentimes is caught in an avoidable hinder position.

Half-Lobs and High-Lobs

All three lob serves (half, high, and high-lob "Z") should be playing a vital role in your overall serving strategy, especially with the 5-foot "encroachment" rule again in effect. If the returner now tries to move up and cut the ball off in the air (fly-kill), he risks losing the point by having his racquet break the imaginary 5-foot line behind the service box. Thus, most players wait for the ball to bounce, which dictates a ceiling return if the serve has been hit correctly.

Lobs are the best "second serve" available, and they provide an excellent first serve when you're trying to dictate a ceiling-ball return. In fact, against players who have trouble with shots that come in around shoulder level in the backcourt, lob serves can actually become an offensive weapon by generating setups off your opponent's misdirected return. Don't be misled, though, for as your level of play increases, opponents make far fewer outright mistakes and you'll find that ceiling-ball rallies develop from most lob-serve attempts.

THE HITTING MOTION

Whatever lob serve you intend to hit, including the high-lob "Z," strive for a stroking pattern without any explosive movements, such as a snapping of the wrist or an extension of the elbow. Hit with a locked wrist and a semi-bent arm motion so that the only "moving" part is a smooth shoulder motion. This should produce a consistent serve, providing you practice the stroking motion and concentrate on hitting your proper front-wall targets.

When working on your motion, try to make contact about waist to shoulder level with a smooth, easy stroke. (High-lob "Z's" require a fraction more power to make the ball carom to the opposite side wall.) Letting the ball drop low will force you to bend down and hit up, while using wrist action to get the right timing. Nothing says you can't have success with this type of motion, but ball contact at shoulder height with a locked wrist is a more *efficient* motion and less likely to fail you under pressure.

Also, keep your non-hitting arm out of the way so that it doesn't limit a smooth motion by forcing you to swing across a barrier.

Here's the nice easy motion needed on the lob serve. Notice the chest-high ball contact, the semi-bent arm, and the locked wrist.

DIRECTION AND STRATEGY WITH THE HALF-LOB AND HIGH-LOB

Hit with the same motion, these two lobs should land about 5 feet behind the service box and angle into your opponent about shoulder-high, thus dictating a ceiling return. You can increase the difficulty of the return by bringing the ball in tight along the side wall—providing it doesn't pop off for a setup. Remember, your goal with a lob is not an ace, but a ceiling-ball return. If you do err, a short lob will at least make your opponent change the direction of the shot.

Even if you're predictable, lob to your opponent's backhand side, unless he has a weaker forehand. You'll find that most players have greater versatility on the forehand side and, if you mis-angle a lob, can hurt you with their return.

The reason you want the ball to land on or near the imaginary 5-foot line behind the back service line is due to the current rule, which states that an opponent's body or racquet cannot break this imaginary plane until the ball bounces. This negates fly-killing of the serve and forces your opponent to short-hop the ball if he chooses to hit an aggressive return. Short-hopping is a much tougher skill than it appears, for you must have precise timing to hit down offensively on a ball that's rising. If an opponent does short-hop this serve—hoping to catch you off-guard—don't panic; simply adjust to a low-zone coverage position and look for the leftup shot that almost always results.

The High-Lob "Z"

This serve requires exactness in execution and is a bit more complicated than regular lobs because of the walls and angles involved, but it pays off by providing an excellent tactical weapon.

EXECUTION

You must coordinate a correct starting position, the right hitting angle, and sufficient velocity to make this serve most effective. Here's a checklist to review:

- ☐ Stand very close to the side wall as you go to serve so that you can create the desired angles. If you contact the ball near the middle of the court, the ball will angle down the middle and almost always come in short or long off the back wall as a setup for your opponent.
- ☐ Aim for a front-wall target area within inches of the side wall and about three-fourths of the way up. This high, tight angle will allow the ball to travel its optimum path, deep to the opposite side wall.
- ☐ When stroking the ball, bounce it near to your body and

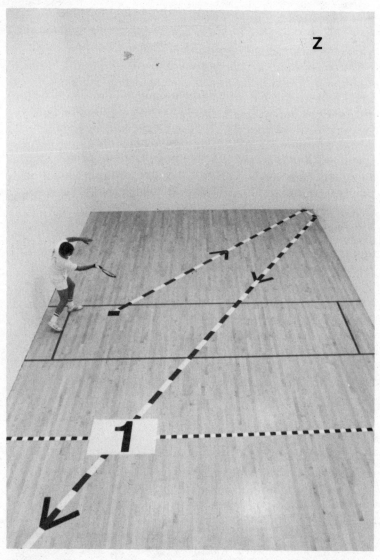

The high-lob "Z" serve takes the basic good "Z" pattern. Notice how far to the left the server must stand. He slides his swing close to his body so he can make ball contact close to the left side wall. It's easier to create the correct angle that way.

A common problem occurs when players make contact too far to the middle of the court and the ball angles down the center.

Some players find it easier to use their backhands to create good ball angles on a high-lob Z to the back left corner. Hit this serve with an easy motion and little or no wrist snap.

try to "slide" the racquet in front of you as you angle the shot up. Swing slightly harder than you do on regular lobs, since the ball must have enough speed to carom across the court and high into the side wall.

☐ On a high-lob "Z" to the back left corner, many skilled players are using a *backhand* stroke with no wrist action, simply to create an easier hitting angle.

☐ Ideally, try to make the ball strike the 5-foot line (behind the service box) so that it takes a high-arcing path toward

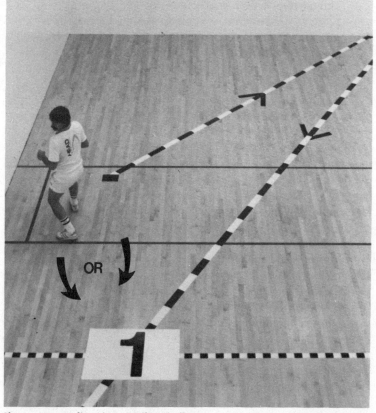

**Since you are dictating a ceiling-ball return with your good high-lob "Z,"
your relocation turn is not so important; your opponent is going up with
the return. But remember, if you mis-hit or he short-hops the serve, you
should adjust your position quickly before it gets dangerous.**

the side wall in the back corner, strikes the wall as high as 6 to 8 feet, and then comes down at a steep angle, just nicking the back wall. This will force your opponent to take the ball to the ceiling, and prevent him from hitting a fly-kill.

☐ Experience—and practice—will enable you to master a relocation turn out of the service box so that you feel secure about watching your opponent set up to hit as you move back. When relocating, you can turn either to the outside or inside, since your goal on the shot is to force a ceiling return. If you execute properly, the return will be directed up and you won't be caught in a precarious hitting lane. However, if you prefer to turn to the inside and your opponent moves up and either short-hops the ball or hits an overhead drive, be ready to turn quickly and adjust your position so you don't get ripped in the nose by an errant shot.

STRATEGY

When a high-lob "Z" comes out of the front corner at the correct angle, it hits the floor and takes a high, steep arc into the opposite side wall. Good sense dictates a ceiling return, either before the ball hits the side wall or just after it rebounds off the side wall, but this poses a tricky execution problem.

On the backhand side, for example, this high arc before the side wall forces your opponent to use a good shoulder swing while taking the racquet face on a more vertical upward pattern than normal, in order to contact the ball effectively. If he has a faulty, arm-poke type of stroke, this could result in numerous setups. Even on the forehand side, the high-lob "Z" can force errors by making your opponent contact the ball at a higher level than normal.

Unless you find a specific lob that negates your opponent's offense practically every time, you will have to mix them up as the match progresses, trying to find which one is the most effective. A smart player also knows that just because his opponent is effective at returning high-lobs to the left corner, this doesn't mean he is necessarily as efficient returning a high-lob "Z" to his forehand.

Regular lobs, for example, are one-dimensional—coming straight down the court—while high-lob "Z's" approach the returner at a different angle and confront him with more of a decision-making process: Hit the ball before the side wall, or wait for it to come off? Yet while high-lob "Z's" may generate more weak returns, there also tend to be more foul-ups by the server because of the angles involved.

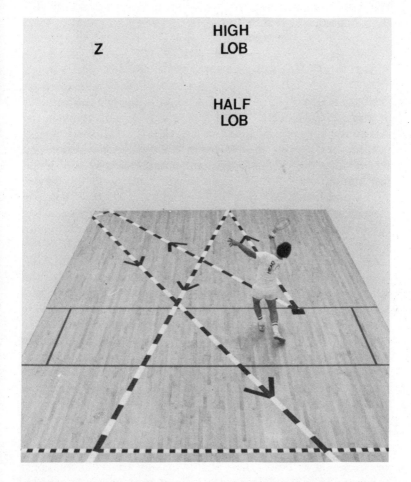

This shows the proper ball direction of the different lob serves. Your goal is to land the serve on the 25-foot line (indicated by the dotted line).

Trying to camouflage your intended lob is much harder to do than on low-drives and hard "Z's," but the high-lob to the back left corner and high-lob "Z" to the back right corner complement each other. Since they are hit from the exact same motion and aimed at the same height up on the front wall, you can be a little deceptive as you mix them up. This helps keep your opponent at bay in the backcourt and makes it harder for him to read where you're serving, which in turn helps keep him from aggressively short-hopping some of these serves.

A Serving Philosophy

Here are some tactical and philosophical thoughts to consider as you pull together a mental approach that will maximize the serves you have in your repertoire.

First, let's assume that you're in a tournament situation and you've never played your opponent before. Obviously, you should test him out early in the first game with a variety of low-drives, "Z's," and lobs to see how well he can return them. If he has a particular weakness, exploit that weakness until he somehow solves the problem; if he can't adjust and you don't give him a reprieve with inefficient execution, you should win. That's the only "strategy" you actually need against an opponent like this.

In reality, of course, as you compete at C-level and beyond against players of relatively equal ability, your opponent will somehow find a way to compensate when you continually serve to a particular weakness. When he does compensate, he's going to start capitalizing on your predictability by "cheating" to certain coverage areas.

That raises a second key point, which is to recognize the importance of having the mental flexibility—and the serves!—to alternate your serving patterns as a typical match progresses or unfolds. I watch many players around the country, at every level, fall into a rut with the serves they have; they use them in predictable ways and they stick with an overall serving style they know best, even if it limits their ability to win against increasingly tougher competition.

Let's say, for example, that when you go in against an unfamiliar opponent you tend to think, "I'm going to pound the ball down this person's throat with low-drives and hard 'Z's.'" Unfortunately, there are those days when your 80-mph serve zips past you as a 100-mph return, continually forcing you onto the defensive. Rather than persist along this suicidal course by thinking, "I just have to hit my serves *harder* and more accurately and I can turn this thing around," you should rather confront your opponent with one lob serve after another, trying to generate ceiling-ball rallies that may help you reverse the momentum.

I lacked this willingness to change from one approach to another when I first began playing, and probably the biggest reason was that I never experimented with different serving styles in practice matches. In tournaments I would always hit a hard first serve and then a lob on the second. I didn't try using lobs exclusively as a first serve to learn the ramifications of that serving style; I was scared to change because I didn't know all the subtleties of a slower game plan created by a lob serve. So I would say to myself, "I'm going to prove to this guy that I can hit low-drive serves come hell or high water." Eventually that stubbornness would cost me the serve, because as good as I might have been at ripping the ball into the back left corner—concentrating on his backhand side—my opponent would begin to realize, "I'm going to move left and play that area because twelve serves in a row have gone there." By anticipating like that as I prepared to serve, he was able to hit low-zone returns that put incredible pressure on me as I relocated.

Here's a similar analogy. If all of your first serves are low-drives to the back left corner, a smart opponent will simply edge over a half step in that direction as you hit—and you may be unaware that he's doing this. If you sense that he's anticipating to this corner, you obviously have a perfect opportunity to ace him down the right side, but only if you've practiced hitting low-drives to that corner. Otherwise you'll be afraid to hit the serve that needs to be hit.

When you have some control of the basic serves, this not only enables you to change game plans as the match warrants, but to initiate the style of play you prefer. For instance, if you favor low-zone exchanges, then emphasize low-drive and hard "Z" serves on the first attempt. When I serve a low-drive to you, for example,

I'm trying to be offensive on the first shot, with a reasonable chance of being offensive on the third shot. I know that a few of my drives will come off the back wall as setups during the match, but otherwise, my aggressive serves will either draw a weak return or force you up to the ceiling. So I'm more likely to have an early scoring opportunity with this approach. Even if you take my serve and return it to the ceiling, I still had the first offensive shot of the rally by hitting a low-drive serve. On the other hand, when I lob to you on the first serve, I'm initiating a ceiling-ball rally and I know that I may not have an offensive shot until the fifth shot of the rally, assuming you return my serve effectively to the ceiling.

In good racquetball, when two relatively equal players go toe-to-toe, the match is a continual cat-and-mouse game between the server and returner. The server tries to keep the returner off-balance with a variety of serves off the same motion, hoping for a weak return, while the returner is looking for any tipoff to get an early jump on the serve. Neither gets to the other with ease.

As a server, therefore, your long-range goal should be to learn to hit your front-wall targets with your basic serves. Don't worry about your opponent "reading" your serve to begin with; make sure you can serve well from appropriate positions. Then you can learn to camouflage your intentions from different parts of the serving zone, while mixing up the serves and directing them into both back corners.

5

The Serve Return

●

Returning serve is a demanding challenge against the good, intelligent server, and your mental approach should be:

- If the serve is weak or mis-angled, be ready to jump on it with an offensive return; make the server pay for his mistake.
- If the serve is simply too tough to shoot, go to the ceiling and patiently wait for a low-zone opportunity.

That's the idealistic plan of attack, but in reality the game situation and how well you're hitting your various shots will dictate just how offensive you can afford to be. After all, if you continually try to be an offensive hero when the opening isn't there, you will simply hand your opponent one setup after another. I find, however, that the majority of players around the country are too defensive when returning serve. They tend to go to the ceiling too much unless they have an absolute setup, bypassing offensive opportunities whenever the server hits a less-than-perfect serve. If this is your approach, you not only give your opponent continual reprieves, you remove the psychological pressure he feels when he knows his opponent is going to hit a low-zone return if his serve is not right on the money.

Ready Position and Readiness

You should take a ready position about 3 or 4 feet off the back wall. This enables you to efficiently cover a good low-drive serve by moving to either side with a strong cross-over step.

The receiver is positioned one step off the back wall to return serve. Most players use a slight drop step to get themselves moving to the side, but the critical part of the return is the crossover step with shoulder rotation. This allows the receiver to reach near the side wall to hit high-zone or low-zone.

Some players take a receiving position as far forward as 10 feet off the back wall. This puts them at a real disadvantage if the server is ripping good low-drives into the back corners, since they are actually moving backward to try to hit a return to the front wall or the ceiling.

A surprising number of players are reluctant to stand this close to the back wall, fearing they will be aced by a low-drive serve that dies up ahead of them. I remind them how difficult it is to hit a low-drive serve that bounces twice inside of 35 feet. Moreover, if you position yourself too far forward, a strong serve will force you to move diagonally backward to return the ball. It's much harder to return the ball offensively when you're retreating diagonally than when you can move laterally from a deeper ready position.

(One exception to this advice. If your opponent's low-drives continually hit too deep and carry far forward off the back wall, then play up another long stride. He's giving you setups and is not going to burn you in the back corner. But remember: You're playing a person who basically doesn't know how to serve.)

When your opponent is serving lobs, you can have a relatively relaxed attitude as you prepare to return serve, since you have plenty of time to move to the shot. But when you have your ready position and you're studying your opponent's serving intentions, you must be keenly alert and ready to react quickly against his low drives and hard "Z's," especially if he knows how to mix them up off the same hitting motion. For example, he might try to burn you with three or four crisp drives into the back left corner that you can barely reach, and then, using the same motion, he suddenly will snap a hard "Z" into the back right corner. This type of serving pressure will cause serious havoc if you're not concentrating and you haven't worked on your serving return skills in practice.

Returning Low-Drive Serves

If you're having trouble covering or just getting the ball back against tough, low-drive serves into either corner, several factors could be holding you back.

First, have you worked on your ability to read the server's intentions? And how soon can you evaluate the serve's effectiveness? Ideally, through experience, you should be able to sense this as soon as the ball becomes visible off the front wall.

Second, you should anchor down in your ready position (but don't let your feet fall asleep!) so that you can move quickly to either side.

Third, an efficient, immediate cross-over step is essential to get you to the ball with enough time to hit. One or two quick shuffle steps will never work.

Keeping these points in mind, when you see a low-drive serve ripping toward the back left corner, your only recourse is to move there with a cross-over step as the shoulders rotate—and then try to flick the ball to the ceiling. Many players can serve a lot of near-perfect low drives, and they play very well when the return is weak and gives them an immediate setup. But it's amazing how inefficient they are and how you can negate their effectiveness when you pull them into a ceiling-ball rally and force them to earn the point within that type of rally.

Generally, against a strong server who mixes up his offensive serves, you should position yourself in the middle of the court and simply be ready to react to either side. But in specific game situations, such as when you need to somehow change the momentum, try gambling a bit. Here's an example.

At one of my 1984 summer camps, I played an exhibition match against an aspiring young pro who happened to be visiting. In the first game, he moved ahead 9–2 (we were playing to 11), and I had the serve. I had been struggling the whole game, but suddenly I started to get a run of points strictly off low-drive serves to the left corner. I kept exploiting that shot until I had won, 11–9. Afterward, I told him that I felt he had made a strategic error while returning serve in that particular game. "You were getting to the ball," I said, "but all you did was go to the ceiling and hope that I would miss and give you a setup. But I had the better ceiling ball and you kept giving me a shot to end the rally." I suggested that instead of reacting defensively to all my low-drive serves, he should have gambled several times. He had nine points and he just needed to get back in the service box to pick up the final two. "I wasn't serving to the right corner because I had found an area I could exploit, so if you had cheated to the left, you could have ripped away at a couple of my tough serves and perhaps broken my momentum. So what if you had missed them both? You would have still been ahead. Instead, you sat back and let me control the play, hoping that I would finally make some errors, but I got grooved in. You let me change the whole momentum of the game and you didn't do much to negate it."

Returning Hard "Z" Serves

Not until you understand each category of the hard "Z" and its return options can you confidently return these serves without being confused and tentative in your reactions.

As a refresher point, remember the server's goal. He wants the ball to go front wall, side wall, bounce on the floor at 25–27 feet, kick into the opposite side wall about 4 feet high, and not come off the back wall. If he generates that kind of an angle, it leaves you two options on your return (assuming here that it's to your backhand; the principles are the same on the forehand):

1. You can take the shot after the bounce and before the side wall and either go low or high, depending upon how ready you are for the shot, how tough it is, and the effectiveness of your backhand. Your closeness to the left wall shouldn't really be a factor.

2. When you're forced to let a good hard "Z" travel into the side wall, the ball can get tight into the back corner and challenge you to dig it out without being aced. In most cases, just be pleased if you can manage to pop a decent shot to the ceiling. When the ball gets so tight to the back wall that you can't execute a ceiling-ball motion, drive the ball into the back wall to keep it in play— but only as a last resort. An alert opponent will simply move up quickly to cut this weak shot off as it comes off the front wall, and will drive it or pinch it low-zone before you can recover.

An unbelievably important fact to understand is that as often as you think your opponent is hitting "perfect" hard "Z's," the majority of these serves are actually short, long, or mis-angled. So what counts is your ability to distinguish the relative effectiveness of your opponent's serve as it comes out of the front corner, and your knowing where you should locate to hit your return. This knowledge removes a lot of anxiety and should keep you from rushing needlessly to the side wall or to the back corner as soon as you see a hard "Z" coming.

The *short "Z"* generally occurs when the serve hits too tight into the side wall and oftentimes a little low. If you can read this serve pattern early, and you're patient, you'll find that the ball will

Off a well-angled hard "Z," the receiver has two options. Since the ball is not coming off the back wall for a setup, he can either hit after the first bounce and before the side wall (photo 1) or after the side wall and before it dies shy of the back wall (photo 2).

If you're faced with an effective "Z" that comes off the side wall nearly parallel to the back wall, here's the correct method for digging this serve out of the corner. Your back foot is basically parallel to the back wall as you slide your racquet through, close to the body. Then pull through with good shoulder motion, extending the arm and snapping the wrist.

Against the tough hard "Z" hit to either back corner, move close to the back wall, slide your racquet parallel to the back wall, and then flick the best possible defensive return with your arm and wrist action.

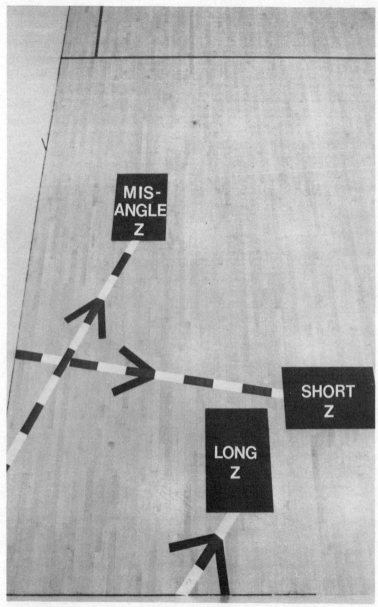

This photo shows where you should stand to return each of the missed hard "Z's." As you learn to read your opponent's "Z's," you will know where to position yourself for the return.

If the receiver has a basic understanding of the short "Z" serve, and the patience to let it run its course, the serve will rebound right to him off the left side wall. Notice how the server must move off to the right side to give the receiver his proper hitting lanes (photo 1). Many players fail to move far enough aside as they relocate, and block the receiver's hitting lane— an avoidable hinder— (photo 2).

A long "Z" will kick off the back wall for an offensive setup (photo 1). The receiver is often afraid that the ball won't come out of the back corner, but the long "Z" serve will always jump off the back wall. So it takes patience not to panic on this return. Photo 2 shows what happens when the server fails to move far enough to the right and creates an avoidable hinder.

The mis-angled "Z" serve either comes directly off the back wall for a setup or off the back wall and then the side wall (as the photo shows). Many players like to hit this return after the first bounce and before the back wall—but as you can see, when the receiver lets the serve run its course he ends up with an easy setup.

rebound close to your original ready position—so stay put. The server must now relocate off to the right to allow you to drive the ball straight to the front wall and pass him down the right side if you choose. Your obvious shot is down the open left lane, but the server must still give you these other hitting lanes.

The *long "Z"* serve travels the desired angles, but jumps off the back wall as a setup. However, you must patiently wait for all this to happen, for when you see the pattern develop, you immediately think it's going to be such a good serve you won't even get a return. But right at the end, the ball rebounds off the back wall on a diagonal. You must learn to read this angle and let the ball drop low, then go for the offensive return.

The *mis-angled "Z"* occurs when the ball hits the front wall too far away from the side wall and proceeds to angle down the middle of the court. Depending upon how badly the serve was mis-hit, the ball will either rebound directly off the back wall for a setup, or carom into the back wall and then off the side wall. When you read this pattern early, let the ball run its course and then be ready to go low-zone with your return.

Returning Lob Serves

A good lob serve will come in to you at shoulder height, short of the back wall, so a ceiling shot is your soundest return option. Instead of risking a leftup shot by trying to pull the ball down, go to the ceiling and wait for a better offensive opportunity. Your opponent initiated this high-zone type of rally, and keeping it from paying off for him is what gains you respect on the racquetball court.

When you play the methodical opponent who loves to serve nothing but lobs, and you don't want to get caught up in endless ceiling-ball rallies, you must learn to "read" his slightly off serves and take the offensive. You can also try to short-hop the half-lobs that normally dictate a ceiling return. This is a difficult skill to acquire, but one you can work on. Simply have a friend hit half-lobs that land at about 25 feet so that you can move up and practice short-hopping the ball and driving it low into the front wall. Once you can do this in a match and keep the ball off the back wall, I guarantee that you will force your opponent to either react quickly in center-court or retrieve outside of that area.

Against the high-lob, you can try to avoid a ceiling-ball rally by hitting an overhead drive from shoulder level, but we know how difficult this is, and if you give a good player nothing but setups, you can count on seeing one lob serve after another—especially if you also are inefficient in high-zone exchanges. You may also be tempted to move up and short-hop the ball just behind the back service line and drive it low. But over the years, I've seen very few players who could do this consistently and not leave the ball up as an easy setup. You may be able to do this in practice, but can you pull it off at 8–8 in the tie-breaker?

Defending Against the High-Lob "Z"

The high-lob "Z," when properly hit, will land deep and take a high arc to the side wall, then die before coming off the back wall. If this serve has been hit to your forehand side, the tendency is to think there should be a return shot that can immediately win the rally. "I should be able to hit a shot that negates everything the server is trying to do here," is the thought going through your head. In reality, however, these are your options:

1. You can try to short-hop the ball after it contacts the floor, and attempt to score or drive your opponent out of center-court. This looks easy but is quite hard to do, and your opponent should be ready to jump on any leftup shot.

2. You can take the ball between the bounce and the side wall and go to the ceiling (generally the wisest choice), or try to hit an overhead drive, particularly on the forehand side. Once again, though, you must be able to execute to put the server on the defensive.

3. You can take the ball between the side wall and the back corner and go to the ceiling.

4. You can wait, and gamble that you can shoot the ball when it comes off the back wall, but that's not going to happen if the serve has been hit right; the ball will die just as it reaches the back wall.

When you do go to the ceiling, you had better prove at least equal to your opponent in a ceiling-ball rally. Otherwise he is

When you return a high-lob "Z," you can make contact either before or after the ball hits the side wall. If the serve is effective, your return will usually go to the ceiling.

An effective way to create a low-zone rally against an effective high-lob "Z" is to "overhead drive" the return.

probably going to exploit you in this one area of the game. You may beat him elsewhere around the court, but if he's serving high-lob "Z's" he's trying to create high-zone play. When you face an opponent like this and you're thinking, "I don't like the ball coming back in high all the time; I can't win rallies when we go to the ceiling," then you must work on the shots that will put some low-zone pressure on your opponent (for example, short-hopping, or an overhead drive off his high-lob "Z"), and also spend time working on your ceiling-ball game.

Practice and Improvement

When you practice, try to seek out a player of similar ability who can hit you the respective serves. A good approach is to alternate serving ten serves of one type to each other, where you play the rallies out and then change serves for the next ten. That gives each player the same number of returns and nobody monopolizes a position. Changing servers like this is also good for practice improvement because you eliminate keeping score; both players can then work on shots without the fear of every miss going against them.

If you don't have somebody to hit you serves, which is most often the case in this sport, then learn to toss the ball toward the back corner from your ready position and practice going for the different type returns. This drill may sound simplistic, but it can be quite effective.

Another way to raise your effectiveness when returning serve (especially if you realize you currently have an overly defensive strategy) is to consciously start shooting more balls in practice matches, even if you give your opponent one setup after another. Be patient but persistent in this transition stage to a more offensive style of play, for many times you will be tempted to simply go to the ceiling rather than lose yet another quick point. If you're not willing to suffer a few losses along the way, improvement might be hard for you.

Eventually, this change you're making is going to pay off as you learn how to put pressure right back on the server by being aggressive and not letting him slip off the hook when he misses his serve.

These players are using a good method to improve their cross-over steps and serve returns.

This same drill can be used effectively by one person. Notice the easy underhand toss.

Notice how the receiver has been thrown off-balance in the left corner after a low-zone return, but uses the left wall to push himself back into play.

6

Court Coverage

●

Good racquetball play demands that you continually make the transitions between low-zone action and high-zone exchanges, hitting and covering as efficiently as possible. In Chapter Three, I discussed coverage tactics in relation to high-zone rallies. Now I want to focus on ways to be a savvy defender in offensive situations.

When defending in a low-zone rally, this should be your thinking process as your opponent prepares to shoot: "I'm watching the ball and studying my opponent, trying to anticipate the shot he's going to hit, but my main concern is to be ready to cover his leftup shot." This in turn should dictate a basic, desired coverage position starting at about 24 to 27 feet against nearly all the players you'll encounter at any level of play. Here's my logic.

First of all, one of five things must happen when your opponent shoots the ball low-zone:

1. Skip.
2. A kill that dies in front of you (but a shot you try to contest with one good step forward if possible).
3. Two bounces before the back wall.
4. One bounce before the back wall.
5. No bounces before the back wall.

Before you read on, ask yourself, "Which one of these five options do I play off when my opponent shoots the ball?" Realistically, you'd better be playing off possibility number three since

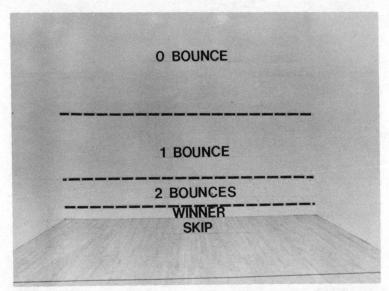

When covering your opponent's offensive shot attempt, remember that your coverage will depend upon how high he hits the ball into the front wall. The skip is a gift, and you can't cover the winner. Of the three options left, "two bounces" is the hardest to cover, so you must condition yourself to play off the shot that will take two bounces before the back wall.

this type of shot can hurt you more quickly than the other *playable* shots. You can't control the destiny of the first two options—skips and kills—and you'll have time to hit the last two options as they come off the back wall.

You should always play off your opponent's leftup shots. And since most players hit with reasonable velocity, this means the ball is going to be traveling deeper far more frequently than you might imagine. As a result, you should concentrate on playing as efficiently as you can in the *back half* of the court, while conceding the front 15 feet. Virtually every playable shot will funnel back here in the course of a typical match—at the novice level right on through the pro level. If you're skeptical, carefully watch a match at your club and count how many shots are taken from behind the service zone as opposed to the front half of the court during the rally (not counting the serve and the return). Or, chart any match and compare the shots that bounce twice inside of 15 feet versus

When covering your opponent's low-zone attempts, keep reminding yourself to play off his leftup shots.

the ones that travel deeper. You'll see for yourself that kills are vastly outnumbered by leftup opportunities.

My emphasis on a deep coverage position may challenge your conviction that racquetball is a "kill shot" game, but deep coverage should form the bedrock of your defensive thinking; it is the most correct and efficient way to cover shots in a low-zone rally if you want to have a consistency in your positioning and be in a prime area to rescore on as many of your opponent's leftup shots as possible.

The Virtues of a Deeper Position

By positioning yourself at about 24 to 27 feet (or a bit closer to or farther from the front wall, depending upon your opponent's actual shot-making abilities and the specific situation in the rally), you concede your opponent the kill up in front, but meanwhile you're in excellent position to play off his many leftup shots. You'll have more shots coming to you than you ever believed possible, and with a strong step forward from 26 feet, you can still possibly get your racquet on a ball at 20 feet. If he puts the ball down too

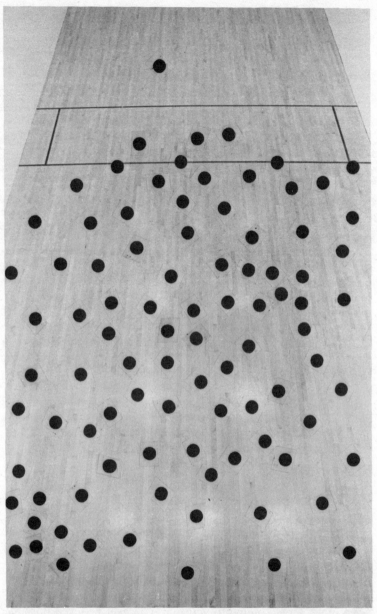

The dots on this court indicate where each shot was hit during a match rally, after the serve and return. Have a friend chart one of your matches and you'll realize why you must concentrate on covering shots in the 20-by-20-foot action area behind the service zone.

far in front of you, then he hit a good shot and deserves the point or side out. You can acknowledge his good shot, but silently tell him, "You better keep doing this because when you start missing, you're going to pay."

Another benefit of the deep coverage position is the psychological pressure you place on your opponent, for you're basically telling him, "If you kill the ball, you're going to get your points, but if you leave it up even slightly, I'm ready to re-kill."

When you come into a match against an opponent you've never played before, and you stay back to cover his leftup shots and to re-kill them, I guarantee that this will have an immediate effect on his confidence, especially if he understands racquetball. When he leaves the ball up just a bit and you're ready to cover and re-kill, his front-wall target area is going to shrink fast as he feels the pressure to execute.

When you're confident about staying back and playing off the leftup shots, you can adjust objectively to different players. For example, instead of panicking when an opponent you've never played before starts pinching a couple of winners and you think you should immediately move up and cover from near the 20-foot line, you should have the patience to make him prove this skill repeatedly as the first game progresses. Then if he shows a consistent pattern of well-executed pinches, creep up into a closer coverage zone and see if he has complementary shots that can blow the ball by you. If he doesn't, simply camp up there and take away his trusted scoring shot—the pinch.

You will also want to "cheat" closer up, at a strong level of play, when you've given your opponent a relatively easy, off-the-side-wall setup at around 25 feet and he has been scoring consistently with this type of shot during the match. You should respect his ability here by moving up to about 21 or 22 feet.

Once a match begins, try to sense where most of your opponent's low-zone shots are taking a first bounce. He may be an aggressive player who impressively rips the ball, but is he putting it down? He could be taking tough, low-percentage shots that will continually kick back to you—*if you lag deep*. Club players are amazed when they watch videotape of the pros and can see for themselves just how far a hard, low shot (8 to 10 inches up on the front wall) will travel before taking its first bounce. Even more of a revelation is where the second bounce occurs—at 30 feet! We've watched shots hit 6 inches high on the front wall that take their second bounce at 24 feet, for the simple reason that velocity carries the ball deep.

The Limitations of Positioning Too Close to the Front Wall

You will not become a solid racquetball player if you think you must cover your opponent's low-zone shots from near the back service line, give or take a foot. When you play too far forward like this, you're preoccupied with kill shots and you stifle your playing potential in several ways.

First, instead of minimizing your opponent's winners by trying to be a retrieving hero, you're actually giving him *more* opportunities to win the rally. You may dig up an occasional kill attempt that is slightly too high (around the 15-foot area), but the best you can usually hope to do with the ball is flick it somewhere to the front wall or the ceiling. And if your opponent does leave his shot up, the ball can easily jam you in center-court and force a weak return.

A practice suggestion. Have a friend watch or videotape one of your matches so that you can determine where most of your opponent's low-zone shots are taking a first bounce. This will give you an objective understanding of where you should be positioned in a low-zone rally. If you're currently playing too far up and your opponent's scoring shots are hitting 2 or 3 feet high on the front wall, then the ball is taking its first bounce at around 21 or 22 feet—right near where you're standing. Move back closer to 27–30 feet and you'll be positioned where these same shots bounce to you at knee-to-waist height, in the best possible arc to hit low again.

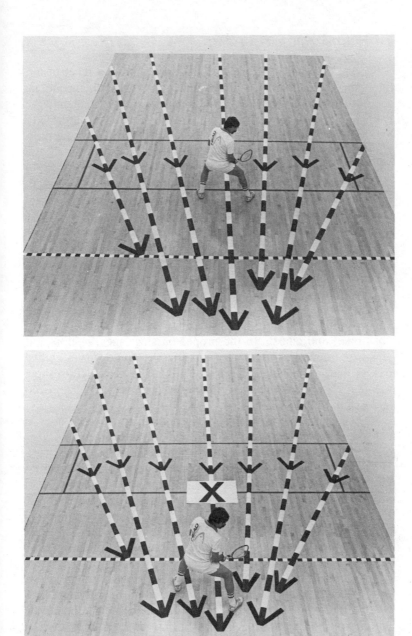

When players cover too far forward, they get jammed by shots coming straight off the front wall. Many shots also get around and behind them (photo 1). So learn to cover at about 24 to 27 feet, for this is where most center-court action occurs. (The dotted line is 25 feet from the front wall.)

Second, playing up close like this forces you to react faster, often simply by instinct, and this makes it tougher to execute an accurate low-zone shot. You're in no man's land too often, and the ball will be continually bouncing near your feet and forcing you to half-volley shots—a difficult skill for anybody, including the pros. Unless you have incredible reflexes and racquet control, all you end up doing is short-hopping the ball (at best) and punching it to the front wall, giving your opponent another setup. If you're covering from 20 or 21 feet and telling yourself, "Cut it off, cut it off," you're setting yourself a most difficult task, since the ball's hitting at your feet. As a result, you can't really cover what your opponent kills, nor can you effectively cover what he leaves up, and this could explain why you find yourself in deep trouble trying to play center-court.

Third, while playing up near 20 feet may intimidate certain opponents, an experienced player will pick you apart—without having to kill one ball to do it. After he gets used to where you're positioned and adjusts to the proper passing lanes, he'll exploit you with accurate wide-angled passing shots and down-the-line passes that hug a side wall. Meanwhile, many of his leftup shots will jam you, and some of his real mis-angles will get behind you and go for winners.

I once had a fellow at my summer camp in Aspen who was conscientious about his game and had worked diligently to become a B player, but he was totally indoctrinated in the kill shot. He wanted to improve his playing level, and he thought he had to kill more balls, serve more aces, and cover more kill attempts in order to compete against the players who were slightly above him. He also felt that as he advanced into better play, his opponents would be killing the ball constantly, and he didn't want to give up those points uncontested; he felt he had to position himself near the service zone, ready to dig those kills up.

So we had to totally re-educate him, which was tough on his ego; he had been programmed to play a certain way for about two years. But when he saw his game analyzed on videotape, he admitted, "You know what? I didn't think this game out right at all." That was a disappointment for him, but it was certainly better to learn about these shortcomings than never to realize that they were holding him back from reaching a higher level of play. Without re-education, he never would have attained that higher level because he didn't have the right objectives in mind.

Watching the Ball and Your Opponent

At my winter and summer camps, we spend a lot of time encouraging people to follow the ball between shots and to study their opponent's stroke right up until contact—*then* to turn to the front wall and react. Many players are either unaware of just how much information they can gather by doing this, or they're afraid of being hit in the face by the ball, so they square to the front wall too early. As a result, they minimize their chances to anticipate their opponent's shot, and this forces them to continually lunge for low-zone attempts or frantically retreat against a ceiling ball.

How well do you keep your focus on the ball and try to read your opponent's intentions? If you actually watch him set up to hit and start his swing—instead of simply glimpsing him out of the corner of your eye—you'll know if he's shooting or going to the ceiling, and you can quickly move into an appropriate coverage position. Learning to interpret his body motion and racquet action will take away much of the guesswork in your coverage.

When a player begins to watch the ball and his opponent, he is often amazed at the results. The typical response is reflected by the letter I received from a camper: "You would be pleasantly surprised to see how my game has improved since camp. . . . I'm following the ball much better, but must consciously work on it all the time. My floor coverage is much better and my endurance seems to have improved." Actually, his endurance had improved because he was more efficient in his court coverage. By watching the ball, he could anticipate where his opponent's shot was going and thus reach more shots. Before that, he would stand with his eyes glued to the front wall whenever his opponent was hitting from behind him, and he couldn't react until he saw the ball come off the front wall; then he had to make a mad lunge to cover. Scrambling like this throughout a match will wear anybody down.

If you're not reading your opponent's swing, and are continually reacting to balls *after* they come off the front wall, this could explain why your game has not been improving. You can't afford to react this late to shots as you try to move up in this game.

Jerry Hilecher has turned correctly and is watching Gregg Peck set up for his offensive backhand. Jerry, positioned at about 25 feet, is ready to cover a leftup shot.

Mike Yellen is covering Jerry Price's low-zone backhand attempt at about 24 feet. In top pro play, 24 feet is an appropriate coverage position against a player with Price's offensive potential. In good B-level play, where the hitter is less consistent putting the ball down, 27 feet would be a sensible coverage distance.

One caution: While recommending that you look back at your opponent as he goes to hit, I'm also assuming that you wear eye guards. I played without them for a while, like most of the pros, because I felt, "I know he's not going to hit me." But then I realized, "What if he **does**— just once?" Playing without eye guards is not worth the risk, and the fear of getting hit in the eye will cause you to turn away from your opponent too soon.

Etiquette and Coverage

Racquetball players should have a mutual respect for each other as they hit and as they cover. This results in a clean, competitive match that is also safe for both players. Two key issues are involved here.

First, *give your opponent room to swing.* I tell all my students, "If you get hit by the racquet, it's your fault." This helps motivate them to stay clear as their opponent swings, especially in center-court action. Also, when you get caught against the wall, stay there long enough to let your opponent swing. If he has to hold up because he sees you moving into his path, that's an avoidable hinder. (The other half of the responsibility is for the hitter to shorten his backhand follow-through in center-court so that he doesn't nail his opponent.)

Second, *give your opponent the proper hitting lanes.* Be assertive in assuming your coverage position, but also be reasonable, for you must give your opponent room to hit a straight-in shot to the front wall, a cross-court pass to your side of the court, and a pinch into the nearest front corner. This is another reason why you should turn and watch the ball and your opponent after you hit, so that you can position yourself accordingly.

When you and your opponent give each other clearance to hit, the match will run pretty smoothly (even though both of you may be quite subtle at closing off one of the passing lanes). Unfortunately, as we all know, many players are stubborn about moving aside, or they don't understand that the defender is guilty of an

Notice how the offensive player shortened up his backhand follow-through in center-court for the safety and protection of his opponent.

avoidable hinder when he fails to give the hitter the proper hitting lanes. As a result, we have to learn to live with all these avoidable hinders until many more players are willing to abide by the spirit of the rules. Until then, the problem—at all levels—is spoiling a lot of good racquetball play.

A Checklist: Defensive Play

☐ Understand the areas on the court that you can cover with reasonable efficiency.

☐ Understand your opponent's scoring areas.

☐ Be ready to play off your opponent's leftup shots, rather than trying to play off his kills.

☐ If your opponent becomes too predictable in his shot selection, "cheat" into his favorite lanes/zones/areas until he makes the proper adjustments.

☐ When you are in a low-zone rally, your coverage position should fluctuate between 23 and 30 feet, depending on the type of shot your opponent is hitting and his ability to execute that shot.

☐ Watching the ball at all times will greatly increase your readiness to cover your opponent's next shot. (If you do not watch the ball, you will reach a plateau in your anticipation and your game will not improve.)

☐ Wear eyeguards for your protection and confidence.

☐ Give your opponent the proper hitting alleys, but don't give up *too much* court trying to avoid getting hit by his shot or racquet.

☐ Keep adjusting your feet up until the last moment so that you're in the best possible position to hit.

Improving Your Movement and Coverage Abilities

Racquetball doesn't require you to have a sprinter's speed as you cover the court, but it does emphasize having reasonably strong legs and quickness, as well as the endurance to weather long rallies—and two-hour matches when you're in a tournament, or another competitive environment. "Court sense" is also needed to pull together your coverage skills and allow you to play efficiently. So here are some drills and tactics that can help strengthen your body and improve your overall coverage ability.

1. Learn to use my 30-second drill (page 195), where you rally by yourself into the front wall, keeping the ball in play and your feet moving. This is excellent practice for your strokes, footwork, and reactions—and for pulling them all together.

2. Do some "shadow movements" without a ball, such as a cross-over step from center-court·to both walls (ending with an actual stroke) or moving diagonally to the back corners. Also practice thrusting forward with one strong step, pretending you're moving up to cover a missed kill attempt.

3. A weight-training program, jumping rope, and running wind sprints will all increase your leg strength and help you get into good *racquetball* shape. Some people run two miles every other day to increase their endurance, some do Nautilus and aerobics, others just play as much racquetball as they can fit into their schedules.

4. One reason many players lack racquetball endurance is that they are not forced into long rallies by their regular opponents or their particular style of play. They play "kill shot" racquetball, always going for the winner but inevitably skipping far too many shots, and few rallies last more than three or four hits.

Therefore, make sure your matches include opponents who understand the subtleties of a good racquetball game. A player like this will move you around the court and inspire long rallies because he doesn't skip the ball in, so be ready for a marathon match where you are forced to execute while having a hard time breathing—exactly the kind of experience you need to toughen you for a tournament tie-breaker.

Gregg Peck uses a good cross-over step and a strong reach to retrieve a ball along the side wall. Crossing over like this is the only quick and effective way to move from the middle of the court to the side wall to cover a shot.

Some players cover the cross-court pass by moving laterally to the shot (photo 1). This is unreasonable, since the ball can travel much faster and will often get by the defender. Subsequently, the defender must try to recover by driving the ball into the back wall. The better option would be for the defender to move diagonally to the right corner (photo 2) and meet the ball there, where he has several offensive options (photo 3).

5. Learn to keep adjusting your feet as you prepare for the approaching ball so that you're in the best possible position to hit—the ball doesn't crowd you by getting too close or end up too far away, forcing you to lunge at the last instant. Many times, of course, a quick exchange of shots in center-court will force you to simply react and hit, without a chance to do much with your feet. Yet in most low-zone rallies, there's enough time to at least take a couple of little steps to get into a better hitting position.

If you study your game on videotape and realize you are standing around too much, then you must reprogram yourself to *always be ready to move,* right up until you're ready to hit. Far too often, I see players take a position and then hope the ball comes to them, especially when it is traveling off the back wall. They seem to be thinking, "Come on ball, I'm here," but when they get planted like this, they must accept what happens if the ball doesn't come to their chosen location. Generally, they are forced to reach behind them to hit, and the result is usually an ineffective shot off the side wall.

6. Keep your feet moving between shots, but remember to get into a set coverage position in or around center-court as your opponent makes ball contact. Some players keep moving forward when their opponent is setting up to bomb a leftup shot, and by failing to locate in one area, they're unable to react with either crossover shuffle steps or a long stride when the kill attempt fails.

7. After you hit, watch the ball and study your opponent's intentions as he goes to hit. Remember, good anticipation is going to help you cover the court more efficiently, with less frantic, scrambling effort as the match progresses.

8. Fight for every point, and when you hit a crummy shot, don't assume your opponent is going to hit a sure winner. If you concede the rally—forgetting that leftup shots far outnumber kills at every level—and fail to relocate to an appropriate coverage position, then you won't be prepared should your opponent indeed miss his "plum" setup, and you'll lose the point anyway.

Other players make the opposite mistake here. After hitting a weak shot, they rush up to the back service line to cover the kill attempt, forgetting the basic philosophy about covering this type of shot. As a result, if their opponent leaves his kill attempt up, they are jammed or the ball goes easily past as an irretrievable pass.

9. While it's important to contest every retrievable shot, *stay on your feet*. Diving for the ball is a bad habit to develop, because it's too hard on your body and you waste valuable time getting to your feet when you should already be adjusting your position. I've seen several pros who are great divers, but after watching them on videotape, I feel they could have more efficient coverage if they learned to stay on their feet. Better to watch pro Mike Yellen, who probably covers better than anybody who has ever played the game. He doesn't dive for anything except as a last-resort effort. He simply relies on strong cross-over steps, quick shuffle steps, and anticipation.

7

Coping with Different Playing Styles

●

Around the club, by carefully selecting your regular opponents, you can usually avoid those personalities and playing styles that seem to bring out the worst in your own game. The only drawback to this approach is that it's easy to fall into a comfortable rut where you rely on one basic playing style—against whomever you happen to play—and you live or die with that particular style. Falling into this rut will haunt you if you venture into league play, try to move up the challenge ladder, or enter tournaments, where you can't avoid those opponents who drive you crazy by forcing you out of your desired playing style. For example, unless you plan to default, you can't chase down the tournament director after your first game against a particular opponent and say, "I'm sorry, but I refuse to play against a guy who hits only lob serves and ceiling balls."

This chapter will give you some tips on how to cope—and adjust your shot selection—against opponents with well-defined playing styles. I'm not providing a rigid strategy to follow against these opponents, since the basic principles of good racquetball apply no matter who you play. But as you compete, there are subtly different shot-making approaches that can capitalize on an opponent's vulnerable areas.

If you are pursuing the tournament rounds, or simply concerned about raising your playing level as high as possible, then you must arrange practice matches against players with contrasting playing styles. You need this experience for a number of reasons:

1. To reinforce the idea that you can't play the same way against every single player—and always expect to win. You must be flexible and adjustable.

2. To give you a keener, more realistic understanding of just what changes you may have to make in your strategy, shot selection, and thinking process to become a better player.

3. To minimize those panic situations when you suddenly have to cover shots you've rarely or perhaps never encountered before. For example, during a ceiling-ball rally your opponent may hit an around-the-wall ball just to see how you handle it. This could prove frustrating if you haven't practiced against this shot; if you've seen it in matches before and you know how to defend against it, though, it's no big deal. Or, let's say that your opponent suddenly starts serving a high-lob "Z" to the right corner and you don't know how to return it. If you panic and your opponent sees that you're floundering with the return, you are likely to see nothing but high-lob "Z" serves. But if you know the options and you've learned through experience that you should basically go to the ceiling rather than try to do too much with this shot, then you can remain calm and calculating.

Aside from tournaments and practice matches, other good ways to play a variety of opponents are to throw yourself into the challenge court, join a league, and seek out as many players as you can at your relative level on the club ladder.

The "Up-Front" Opponent

Good players everywhere tell me that one of their toughest opponents is the player—either tall or short—who reacts quickly, locks in his coverage at about 20 feet, and re-kills many of their scoring attempts. He typically has an attitude that the short line is the theoretical heart of the action, so he loves a low-zone rally where he's in the front and you're trying to beat him from behind.

No doubt about it, this type of player can be intimidating with his quick hands and movements, because it appears that he has

When your opponent plays too far forward in his coverage, exploit him with down-the-line and wide-angle passing shots.

the whole front court covered and there's no human way to put the ball down or get the ball by him. Instead of your good pinches going for winners, they become re-kills for him, and he cuts off your regular passing lanes and drills the ball down the opposite side wall or pinches in the corner.

The typical response here is to panic and lose heart, or to

continue simply pounding the ball, trying to hit it as low as possible. If your basic approach to scoring shots is to kill the ball in front of your opponent, then you will simply grow increasingly frustrated as he continues to rescore on your near-perfect kills. What you must realize is that this type of player is actually quite vulnerable to intelligent shot-making, and that you can pick him apart with wide-angle passing shots and down-the-line (kill) passes that hug the side wall. He's forcing you to hit into the front wall at slightly different angles, but his positioning is also making it easier for you to score points with two particular shots:

1. The wide-angled passing shot. When you start hitting your front-wall target area, this specialty shot will quickly make you realize, "This person is really vulnerable." Your goal is to have the shot hit the side wall on the fly at the same distance your opponent is from the front wall (about 20 feet). This kicks the ball behind him as an irretrievable pass—providing you hit it low enough so that it doesn't come off the back wall. Despite what you may think, not even the very best player can vaporize to the side wall in time to cut the ball off. The speed of the shot, when accurately placed, will get it to the correct side-wall target area way before your opponent reaches it. (Adjust your normal, front-wall target area for a cross-court passing shot over just a matter of inches to the left.)

2. A down-the-line (kill) passing shot, inside the doubles line. This shot goes down-the-line (if not killed) and passes back within the doubles alley. No person is quick enough to cover this pass from such an up-front coverage position.

In this situation, forget your pinch shot, unless your opponent starts moving back a bit to counter your shot strategy. Most up-front players tend to stay near 20 feet, stubbornly sticking with the same playing style, even as they go scrambling to defeat.

You may be tempted to hit ceiling balls to drive your opponent back, but this simply prolongs your agony by initiating a defensive stalemate. Eventually, this ceiling-ball rally is going to become a low-zone exchange and your opponent will quickly return to his favorite location, where it will be misery revisited for you unless you can hit your desired passing angles.

A Drill for the Wide-Angled Pass

This is a tough shot to pull off under pressure, so here's a good drill:

Put tape on your side-wall target (where you want the ball to strike coming off the front wall) and place a towel on the floor below the tape as a visual aid, indicating where you want to contact the side wall with your wide-angled pass. Also place a towel where your opponent would be positioned as you hit. Now simulate a game situation where you see if you can drive the ball into the side wall and have it bounce twice before the back wall. If you can do this, your opponent is going to lose any advantage he might have had way up in front court, and you'll start making him pay for his mispositioning. This is a critical shot to learn because you are going to find many players positioned at about 20 feet, closer to the front wall than they should be.

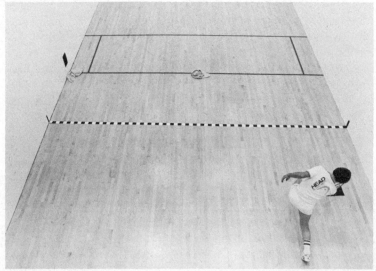

Practice the wide-angle pass by yourself. Simply mark the desired side-wall contact point and use towels to indicate relative locations for your opponent and the side-wall target.

The Lagger

When you play the person who likes to lag especially deep (4 or 5 feet farther back than he probably should), the obvious strategy is to emphasize more pinches and kill attempts into the front court. But beware of the potential pitfalls.

Since your opponent is back slightly too far, you have a little more leniency trying to put the ball down in your low-zone, but not as much as you might think. Also, when your opponent lags deep like this, he's basically tempting you to put the ball down in

Notice how the defender is covering at 30 or 31 feet. Some players would argue that this is excessively deep, but many shots will converge in this area if the offensive player isn't killing the ball. The lagger is thus putting pressure on the hitter to put the ball down.

front of him. So if you think to yourself, "He's deep—I've got to kill it!" you're forgetting just how difficult it is to hit this kind of winner consistently, and you may either skip or leave up a lot of shots—which is exactly your opponent's strategy. And against many players, that's not a bad strategy.

Your opponent also has a good strategy if you normally rely on a passing game and you're not accustomed to putting the ball down. You can try to beat him by driving the ball cross-court and down the line, but you're now trying to hit it around or past a person who is already in the back of the court, and the resulting angles are almost impossible. However, once you start to put the ball down, and avoid the skips, you'll find it a little easier to score points in the front court because of his deeper position.

The Pincher

When I advise people to cover from a slightly deeper position, many of them respond, "Yeah, but when I'm back like that, I get burned by players who soft-touch it into the corners." This will occasionally happen to everybody who plays against an opponent who likes to take velocity off his shots in front court and has good control of his pinches. Such a player will force you to play the front court a little more than normal; you'll need to have a good step forward to dig up shots. But unless your opponent hits the ball perfectly, you will be able to retrieve these finesse shots—and then be offensive.

Meanwhile, you can normally afford to creep up toward the service zone, anticipating his predictable pinch attempts. You may fear that once he gets you cheating up he will start ripping the ball past you, but few "touch artists" have this ability or the requisite flexibility in thinking.

You should also remember that in a low-zone type of rally it is extremely difficult to take the pace off the ball and keep it low; when you can keep the "touch" player hitting on the run, his effectiveness plummets. And when this type of player leaves the ball up, his misses are absolute plums.

If your opponent always pinches the ball, cheat up a little farther in your coverage. Then, with keen anticipation and one good step forward, you can cover even a near-perfect pinch.

The Player Who "Splats"

When you find yourself playing a person who loves to "splat," remember that this shot is nothing more than a spectacular side-wall pinch. It draws a lot of ooh's and aah's when it's rolled out, but results in an easy setup (usually off the opposite side wall) when missed.

If your opponent can kill-pass the ball down the line and cross-court *and* can splat, his ability forces you to play a standard coverage position. For example, when he's near the side wall, he'll be hitting all these low-zone shots off the same motion. Since he can splat the ball as a pinch winner in front of you, he'll force you to cover from about 25 or 26 feet. However, you can often lag back 2 or 3 feet in your coverage if he doesn't have a splat in his repertoire and he's having trouble keeping the ball down.

The typical player who has a fairly strong splat off the backhand side can drive the ball cross-court with the backhand but has trouble taking it down the left wall without erring somewhere along that wall. Since all these misses will kick to the middle, and since the splat and the cross-court pass already travel to the right, you should cheat to the right when playing such an opponent. If your opponent splats predictably into the left wall, move up a bit to cover. But if he is leaving his splats up and mixing in cross-court passes, continue to cheat right but lag deeper.

The "splat" is nothing more than a hard-hit pinch that catches the side wall near the hitter. If your opponent likes to splat and doesn't diversify with down-the-line and cross-court kill-passes, you can cheat up in your coverage and—with a good forward step—cover many of his splat attempts.

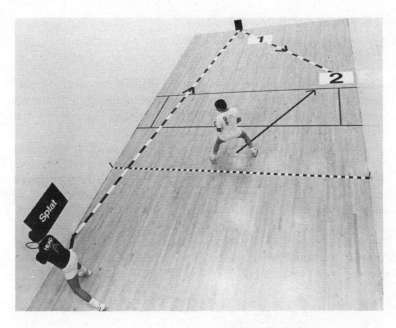

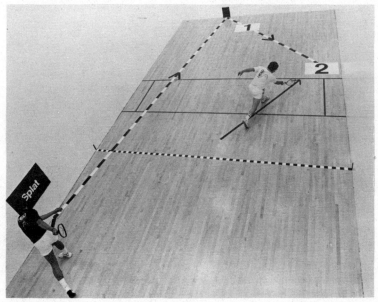

The Lefthander

If you're a righthander whose regular playing partners are right-handed, facing a lefthander in tournament competition can be an unnerving experience. Even lefties have trouble against lefties in a similar situation.

Physiologically, the lefthander doesn't have any advantages in this game, but he seems to have an unwarranted psychological edge on most opponents. For example, I'll often hear a player complain, "I can't seem to play well against a lefty because I'm not familiar with all the hitting angles." The first mistake this player is making is to attempt to hit every possible shot to the lefthander's backhand. Instead, he should simply hit to both sides of the court and the front court with the appropriate offensive

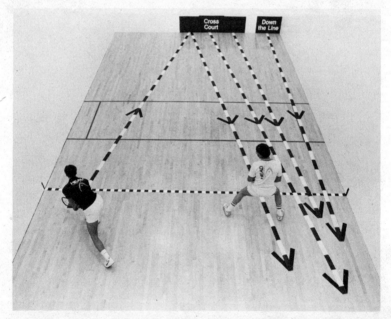

Too many players are conditioned to drive everything to a lefthander's backhand. This predictability in shot selection allows the lefty to cheat to the right. So play it straight with your offense when your opponent is left-handed; hit the open lanes and alleys, whether you're playing to his forehand or his backhand. This diversified attack makes it harder for him to cover.

shots. The second mistake he makes is to flood his opponent's backhand side with an array of serves and cross-court ceiling balls, relying on shots that he has probably overlooked in practice. The result is often an abundance of errors.

Instead of thinking you must change your game plan against a lefthander, just play him like any other player—by going for the logical open shot whenever possible. In a low-zone rally, for example, when you have an open lane down the left wall, take the shot, even though it's to your opponent's forehand.

Meanwhile, practice hitting all your serves into the back right corner so that you're familiar with all the front-wall angles you can use to put appropriate pressure on your opponent's backhand side. There's no avoiding this adjustment in the way you might normally prefer to serve if you plan to be competitive against lefthanders. You might also find a lefty who wants to work on his serve return so that you can practice serving, relocating (looking over your *right* shoulder), and covering balls hit out of the deep right corner.

When hitting cross-court ceiling balls to the back right corner, you may be tempted to hit a perfect ceiling so that your opponent can't even return it. Invariably, however, you'll take too great an angle into the front wall and the ball will catch the right side wall and give your opponent a setup. So practice hitting your ceiling shots safely up the middle of the court to at least force another ceiling ball. Then, as you become proficient, you can begin to edge this shot closer to the side wall.

The Retriever

This type of player is usually a speed demon who scurries all over the court and gets almost everything back. Fortunately, he rarely does much with the ball. He confounds people who play into his hands, but he shouldn't really haunt you if you have considerable patience and a variety of good offensive shots.

The retriever is frustrating to play because he's not going to beat himself—you must beat him with your own shots, patiently over-looking the spectacular gets that deny you one winner after another. Most players tend to panic when their opponent retrieves three or four apparent winners early in the match. They begin to think, "I'm hitting the ball well, but I'm going to have to flat kill it to beat this guy," and they end up skipping their next shot into the floor, trying to be perfect.

What you must remember about the defensive retriever (not to be confused with the strong hitter who has excellent retrieving ability) is that, while he's like a human backboard returning your shots, he seldom tries to capitalize on your leftup shots. Unless he has an absolute plum, he flicks the ball to the ceiling or drives it back to the front wall—giving you another offensive opportunity. For this reason, you must stay cool and collected as you keep pounding away at your low zone; eventually you'll make a shot that he can't retrieve. So what if the rally takes an extra two or three hits to end? It's like target practice. Just be careful not to skip the ball.

This advice is easy to give, but I know how difficult it is to maintain the concentration and persistence necessary to carry it out. The retriever preys on impatience and frustration, and if you're not mentally ready to weather innumerable long rallies, he's going to wear you down and grind out a tough victory. Conversely, when you simply concentrate on hitting your low-zone area, the retriever can continue to track down one ball after another, but you've got him playing *your* game, and, with persistence, you'll win—eventually!

The Ceiling-Ball Artist

If you prefer to play an aggressive, low-zone type of game, you may be frustrated by the methodical opponent who knows he plays best when the game is slowed down. Instead of scurrying around, trying to outblast you, he patiently goes to the ceiling and carefully controls his shot until he's confident about shooting low. Since the ceiling-ball artist will try to draw you into his style of play, here are some tactics you can use to dictate a harder, low-zone pace. (Also see Chapter Three, which outlines tips on how to get out of a ceiling-ball rally.)

1. When serving, rely on low-drives and hard "Z's" to force your opponent to hit quickly and (one hopes) a little off-balance. You're not looking for an ace as much as you are a shot that will make your opponent mis-hit his return slightly. This way you can be offensive and make him scurry to cover your scoring attempt. Your goal is to make him hit his first two shots of the rally on the move, rather than let him set up to hit the way he prefers.

2. When you are returning serve, you have another early opportunity to force the action—except that your opponent will probably hit lob-type serves that force you up to the ceiling. Your immediate recourse, therefore, could be to try to short-hop any lob serve that comes in on target. This is much tougher to do than it looks, but if you're accurate going low zone, you can cause your opponent some serious grief by forcing him to hit quickly and possibly on the move. (If you must go to the ceiling with the return, your ceiling-ball shot had better be good enough to enable you to "hold tough" in the ensuing ceiling-ball rally.)

3. In the course of every rally, keep an aggressive approach overall so that you are continually challenging his coverage skills. This ceiling-ball artist is probably not an efficient opponent in low-zone-type rallies where he must rip the ball, hit on the move, cut the ball off, and so on. He may reach the ball a little late, and will be forced to hit when he's not quite set up, resulting in shots that travel off-target.

One warning, however. Many of these "ceiling experts" can play the other facets of this game reasonably well. They're best when the pace is slowed down a bit, but they can hit effective hard serves, and will look for reasonable opportunities to be offensive. They have the patience to peg out the points, either by punching home your leftup shots for winners or waiting for you to skip the ball if you are careless with your offensive attempts.

The Power Hitter or "Shooter"

Whatever your style of play, you'll need suggestions and strategies to make you more efficient when you go up against an opponent who's obviously thinking "bottom board" on virtually every shot and tries to pound the ball down your throat.

1. You must be mentally ready to be offensive against a serve-and-shoot opponent. If you come into the match a little lackadaisical, hoping to ease into play, you can easily be blitzed in the first game—and never recover. When power players get on a roll, they hit with great confidence and are difficult to contain.

2. Your readiness to play also means that you are mentally prepared to hit shots that are coming at you a little harder (or perhaps a lot harder) than you're used to. We'll assume that you can't hit at your opponent's velocity—but you still must be able to hit with a competitive velocity that can put him on the defensive when you make well-angled, low-zone shots. This means that when he forces you to move to cover his low-zone shot, you're ready to rehit and make *him* move with a good shot. If you're not ready or able to do that, you're going to be retrieving and flicking the ball to the ceiling and the front wall the entire match.

If your basic strategy is to be defensive, and you allow the blaster to dictate an offensive match, you'll be doomed if he's efficient with his shots, for power *with* control will beat control all the time. What you must do is reverse your mental attitude and try to take the offensive whenever the chance is there. Against this type of opponent an offensive outlook may seem suicidal, but it's the only way you can force him to move and hit; many power players are great when they can stand still and shoot, but can be very inefficient when they're pushed into off-balance hitting positions. However, unless you have a determination to be offensive, you'll never know if your opponent has this particular weakness.

3. You can't avoid those little showdowns within a tough rally that force you to go toe-to-toe with a shooter. Even though you may not hit the ball as hard as he does, you can put him on the defensive by hitting accurately within your own limit of power. By doing so, you minimize the number of chances he has to set up and kill the ball.

4. The shooter will get his share of outright winners, and you will too, so the factor that determines who wins will be how well you can handle his leftup shots. Forget about covering the kill attempts that bounce inside of 20 feet, and play off the misses in and around center-court instead. As I've stressed throughout the book, the only disadvantage to hitting the ball hard is that there is such a fine line between keeping the ball down in front of your opponent and keeping it off the back wall. Most shooters rely on the intimidating effect of their power, and they frequently fail to put the ball down as low or as often as we think—and when they leave it up, the ball travels very deep off the first bounce. That's why you should lag back against a blaster, especially when he can't keep the ball down in front. When you camp out at around 28 to 30 feet and tell yourself, "I'm just going to play off the leftup shots," you'll be amazed at how many shots you get that either come through center-court or travel hard off the back wall.

Even the best shooter you know is going to have his off days like everybody else, and his leftup shots will be flooding into center-court. If you're inflexible in your coverage and think you should position yourself at about 23 feet so you can cover all his kill-shot attempts, the ball is going to come to you at a high level in center-court, and will force you into hitting a much more difficult shot than you'd have hit if you had simply moved your basic coverage position back nearer to 28–30 feet. Lagging deeper like this puts *more* pressure on the shooter to try to put the ball down (by being deeper, you are in a much better position to cover his leftup shots). But if the shooter is ripping the ball high and you're staying up at about 23 feet, you will continually get jammed and the shooter will think, "Heck, when I put it down, I know it's a winner, and when I leave it up, he's just flicking it back and not re-killing it." This gives him incredible confidence when he hits.

5. Instead of being intimidated by his power, remember that most shooters (especially the upcoming young players) will give you a lot of points with skips. Also, the shooter may be ripping the ball so hard during warmups that you're ready to concede, but you'll often find that once the match begins, the shooter can't put it together—he can't hit low and he doesn't have a clue where his shots are going.

6. The power player is often quite affected by psychological pressure in tournament play, especially if you don't let him get the upper hand. In regular matches around the club, the shooter is usually relaxed; he's hitting with his maximum power, and his shots are staying down. But very often, once he's in a tournament match, he's like everybody else—he gets fired up, his adrenaline starts pumping, and he tends to be a little less accurate than usual. But he is still ripping hard, perhaps harder than normal, because of the pressure and his eagerness to impress the gallery and his opponent. As a result, his leftup shots are carrying deeper. If you know how to lag deep and cover these misses, the shooter is going to become frustrated at his inability to score; he'll think he's lost his offense and he'll start trying to compensate by over-hitting. He'll try even harder to make those kills happen. The result can be a ton of skips and shots that come to you in center-court and off the back wall. In fact, when two shooters get together and neither player is putting the ball down, the whole match can turn into a back-wall contest.

7. If you are beating the power player, remember that most blasters lack patience and flexibility in their thinking and strategic approach. If a shooter is having an off day and is falling behind, he usually has no alternate game plan; he will tend to simply try to work out his problems by continuing to rip the ball as low as he can. If you're on top of the game, he'll play right into your hands.

8. You can also frustrate most power hitters by hitting shots that dictate a more deliberate tempo and keep them from settling into the fast, low-zone style of play they prefer. When you realize your opponent loves to rip, make sure you give him ceiling balls, lob serves, and high-lob "Z's" at every reasonable opportunity. When you can efficiently execute these serves, you either force your opponent up to the ceiling—if he has the patience—or to gamble on short-hopping the ball. Also, your high-zone shots will force him to adjust to this type of rally, and his impatience may lead to one setup after another as he tries to create low-zone action.

The Intimidator

Ideally, a racquetball match should boil down to execution, coverage, and overall strategy—in other words, "may the best player win." Yet in the real world, you must cope with the occasional opponent who tries to undermine your game with flagrant hinders, constant arguing about calls, unwarranted delays, and verbal outbursts.

This intimidating behavior has a detrimental effect on most players, especially in a tournament situation, for they lack the concentration necessary to overcome or block out the various distractions and disturbances; little irritations begin affecting their emotions while continual interruptions in the flow of play upset their shot-making ability. Most referees fail to take control of the situation by curbing the commotion, and a match can eventually become such a hassle to play that the affected player—the intimidator's target—often loses his original competitive spark and never seems to gain momentum.

If you're determined not to let your game against an intimidator go downhill, your best defense is to keep from showing—through your expressions or by the quality of your play—that his behavior is affecting you. This takes a type of concentration that is difficult to implement, but you'll come out ahead if you try to develop the attitude that you are going to play your own game regardless of how your opponent is acting. Remember, an intimidator's performance tends to remain unaffected—or may even improve—when the match is in turmoil, so if you let his antics negatively affect your own quality of play, it's pretty easy to predict where the momentum of the match will go. If you let these intimidating efforts get to you, your game may go down the tubes even if you have superior talent. I've seen this happen not only at the club level, but on the pro tour, where young kids coming up are intimidated by the veterans.

The "No Hope" Opponent

Then there's the player who just doesn't *look* like a racquetball player and he lulls you into complacency as the two of you warm up. You watch him swing and you're convinced that a racquetball court is simply not his type of environment, and you wonder why he ever signed up for this big tournament you're planning to win. By the time you start, you've already won the match in your mind. But it doesn't take long to realize that his forehand has more power than it did when he warmed up, his serves are right on the money, his punch backhand is causing you trouble, his awkward ceiling stroke somehow yields an accurate hit, and he has a reasonable ability in center-court. In fact, you're playing an efficient racquetball player and he gets the job done so well that he wins the match.

The moral of this story: No matter how inept a person might look while warming up, don't automatically write him off as a player. Just get in there, play your game, nail down the victory, and get out.

8

Improving Your Stroking Technique

●

Now that you've analyzed the shots that need to be hit in good racquetball, you must have an open mind about your stroking technique off both sides (forehand and backhand). The key is: Can you implement the strategy in this book with the strokes that you now have? For example, are you having problems being offensive from the deep court on the left side? If so, you may be punching the ball with only your arm, instead of getting the hips and shoulders into the shot. Do you have an erratic forehand that causes you grief in a fast-paced match? You could be taking an unnecessarily high loop on your setup, which makes it difficult to get the racquet face square at impact.

These are just two examples of where subtle changes in technique—or even a major revamping of your stroke—would be appropriate. If you understand the game but you're uncomfortable hitting certain shots because of faulty technique, this chapter will offer a number of approaches to help bring about improvement.

When teaching the forehand and backhand today, I continue to emphasize the basic fundamentals I illustrated in my previous book, *Advanced Racquetball*. These key concepts help insure a solid stroke that "repeats" itself in the hitting zone, allowing you to hit with power and accuracy even when you're not set up. When you can incorporate these techniques into your swing, the ball will jump off the racquet instead of simply making contact, and even your "misses" will put pressure on your opponent.

The game's top players follow the fundamental swing patterns described here. Their setups and follow-throughs will differ slightly, since people must adjust to the way their own body is structured (some more flexible, others stiff), but down in the hitting zone—from about 2 feet before impact and 2 feet after—the leading players use the same fundamental motions.

The Forehand

The forehand motion is the single most important part of your stroking technique, since it is the basis of most of your offense— for example, your forehand shots in a rally, and your serving motion for low-drives and hard "Z's." Here are four crucial elements that need to be grooved into your swing:

1. The Setup. In my opinion, the best way for you—and virtually all players—to set up is to bring your hitting elbow back up to about *shoulder* level. This will give you enough leverage and time to come down through the ball powerfully and efficiently.

True, you can generate slightly more power by taking the elbow higher (as many elite players do), but lengthening your swing like this requires more precise timing as you try to bring the racquet face through flat at impact. The shooting accuracy lost in this tradeoff is not at all worth it, especially since the real power in your stroke is created by good shoulder and hip rotation, elbow extension, and wrist snap. When you try to take your elbow higher than the shoulder (a physical impossibility for many players), you must also control more movement each time you swing. This may be fine when there's plenty of time to hit, such as when the ball is coming off the back wall, but in better play, you'll realize that you need a more compact stroke in center-court action where the play is quick and demanding.

A high setup is one of several extra elements in a swing that honestly doesn't mean that much, except to the elite players for whom high velocity is critically important and an extra 2 percent in power can make the difference between a winner and a get. You should think, "elbow up to the shoulder," so that your stroke is complete but not excessively long, and then strive for the correct

A good starting position on the forehand, for most players, is to have the elbow at the same height as the shoulder. Many of the top players take the racquet higher, but this takes expert timing, strength, and flexibility. You can rip the ball with plenty of power from the position shown here.

mechanics. Once you acquire a grooved motion, you can learn to add more power *within* the motion.

2. Elbow Extension and Wrist Snap in the Hitting Zone. You may be slight of build, but if you can extend your hitting elbow just before impact—so that your arm is straight—and snap your wrist properly, you will hit the heck out of the ball. Conversely, no matter how strong you might be, you will have serious problems generating velocity if you lack this explosive inner motion, starting about 2 to 3 feet before impact.

This photo sequence shows the important fundamentals. Notice the good elbow bend coming down through the swing and the explosive elbow extension at ball contact. The follow-through pulls around a good distance to give the swing a strong finish.

One summer I worked with an A player from Wisconsin who hit her low-zone shots accurately but at a relatively slow speed, which allowed her opponents to easily track down her shots. This shortcoming was caused by her failure to get a full extension of her arm at impact; she would push at the ball rather than explode through it, so she didn't have enough velocity to blow the ball past her opponent.

In the same way, if you're using your body properly and extending your arm the right way—but failing to fully snap your wrist—then you're not going to generate that extra power needed on your hard serves and low-zone shots. In fact, if you haven't learned to use the wrist snap correctly, you could be losing a large percentage of your potential power.

3. Contacting the Ball. Many players have been told that when they have time to set up on a forehand, they should try to let the ball drop to about ankle height before making contact. This is ideal—if you happen to have the agility of an athletic teenager and precise timing as you hit down through the ball at this level. In reality, I've found that trying to contact the ball this low (6 to 8 inches off the floor) is too demanding physically for the majority of players. Most low-zone shots in a rally will actually be hit in a range between waist height and just below the knee.

When your racquet contacts the ball below knee level, the racquet angle can vary, depending upon how much you bend your knees. The racquet face can be at the same height as the wrist, or tilted below wrist level (this is totally acceptable, and most practical given the difficulty of bending low with the knees to drop the racquet face). When you make contact between knee and waist, the racquet face and wrist should be on about the same level. What counts here, at any level, is how well you can contact the ball with a flat, wrist-snapping action that generates power and keeps the ball low and on target.

Whenever possible, make sure you keep the ball far enough from your body so that you can extend your hitting arm comfortably at contact, giving you that final pop on the ball.

4. The Follow-Through. You can follow-through on a horizontal level, but it's more natural to finish up at around ear level. Also, keep your non-hitting arm out of the way so that you can swing the racquet through freely. Leaving this non-hitting arm across your body forces you to swing across a barrier and will limit your effectiveness.

COMMON PROBLEMS

When you study your swing in a mirror or on videotape, or with the assistance of a teaching pro or a player you feel you can trust, here's a checklist of flaws to look for:

- Relying too much on the arm when swinging, instead of utilizing strong upper body movements tied in with rotation of your hips and legs.
- Straightening or extending the hitting arm *too early* in the swing, which results in an ineffective, tennislike stroke. (This habit is curable, but you must have patience, since early extension is usually so ingrained that it takes hundreds of swings in front of a mirror just to get the arm to go through the desired motion. Also, get on a practice court and just bounce the ball and hit, for as soon as you play again under pressure, the old habit will try to reappear.)
- Your hitting arm is too close to your body, constricting your ability to really pop the ball.
- Not enough wrist snap.
- Stopping the swing too abruptly, which is hard on the arm.
- Your non-hitting arm stays in front of your body during the swing and on the follow-through. (You should dip the hitting shoulder as your initial movement out of the setup position, and have your non-hitting shoulder clear the way as you swing through the shot.)
- Having the off-hand touch and even grab the racquet before the setup, either to help switch grips or to get the racquet set properly. Touching the racquet like this won't hurt your efficiency when there's plenty of time to set up, but it's an unnecessary movement that can cost you points here and there in center-court rallies when you need all the time possible to set and hit quickly. Have a friend watch to see if you've fallen into this habit—or check yourself on videotape—and if it persists, try holding on to your shorts or put a ball in your off-hand as a constant reminder not to touch the racquet handle.

One reason you may be having trouble scoring from center-court is that your non-hitting hand is inadvertently touching the racquet just before you go to swing. There's just not enough time to do this in a fast exchange and still make your shot. People who have this habit tend to hit with a late, punched stroke that limits their offensive potential.

The Backhand

Most players have a two-pronged problem on the backhand, starting with an ineffective swing that limits their accuracy and velocity. This in turn creates a lack of confidence in the backhand, which results in an overly defensive shot selection. Let's go to work on the stroke that you now have and find ways to make it more offensive and reliable.

1. The Setup. Setting up correctly is the key to a strong backhand, for when the elements are in place—racquet back, elbow bent, hips turned, and shoulders rotated—everything will come together successfully at ball contact.

An excellent setup position for most players is to have the hitting shoulder faced into the back left corner, with the hips rotated slightly toward the back wall. This setup creates a swing that has reasonable length but is controllable, with considerable potential for velocity. Players in the elite class may find it necessary to rotate their shoulders until they are parallel to the back wall in order to gain the increased power demanded at that level.

Taking the racquet back high is okay, provided you can pull it down from there and retain good timing. If you're having trouble, set the racquet lower, and you'll still reach the ideal point in the hitting zone.

2. Hitting with Shoulder Action. When you initiate the backswing by rotating your hips and shoulders away from the ball, this should automatically pull your racquet up and back. You should now strive for strong rotating action by the shoulders as you utilize the power in your body to pull the racquet forward, rather than simply "arm" the ball with a punching type of motion.

Too many players try to let their arm do the work instead of rotating into their shot with the hips and shoulders. If this is your problem, remember that even the strongest arm becomes increasingly inaccurate and inconsistent as the match wears on and the arm wearies. You might be able to muscle a lot of shots with a strong arm, but you'll find timing is difficult; one time your arm will come through too quickly and the next time you'll be late in getting it through too late.

Notice how the hitting arm is pulled way back on the backhand setup, and how the top of the arm—from the shoulder to the elbow—is nearly parallel to the floor.

During the swing, there's good elbow bend until just before contact, when the body is pulling through and the elbow is extending explosively.

Good use of your shoulders, however, will relieve the pressure on your arm and solidify your hitting motion by transferring the power demands to your entire body. This will make it much easier for you to hit hard with greater accuracy into your low zone, as you simply concentrate on timing the shoulder action as you rotate through the shot.

3. Contacting the Ball. When you have time to set up, waiting for the ball to come into your ideal hitting zone calls for patience. Let the ball come deeper than you might want to. If you are right-handed, contact the ball off the inside of your left foot. Keep the ball comfortably away from your body so you have room for leverage as you hit. If you contact the ball out in front of your right foot, you are very likely "arming" the ball too much, and losing power and accuracy.

As you rotate into the ball with the hitting shoulder and pull through with your arm, your arm should start to extend, but your wrist remains cocked until you snap through at impact. You want elbow extension and a subtle but strong wrist snap. *Rip the ball,* don't simply reach out and slap or poke at it.

On the follow-through, learn to pull through with shoulder and hip action, but be sure to shorten your swing in center-court before you interfere with your opponent's anticipated coverage position—for safety's sake.

4. The Non-Hitting Arm. Letting your non-hitting hand touch the racquet is much less of a problem on the backhand than the forehand, since you're taking the racquet back in the same direction as the non-hitting hand. However, if this hand inhibits the desired setup by limiting your shoulder rotation or stopping your racquet from traveling back far enough, then this unnecessary habit should be eliminated.

5. Taking the Offensive. An important goal at my camps is to get players to become more aggressive on their backhand sides. They generally have better potential than they think they do, but it's still a tough battle to get them to think of this shot as an offensive one.

If you are too tentative on this side—at your particular level of play—the first important breakthrough, of course, will be to find the weaknesses in your stroke that need to be remedied. Then, in addition to working on an empty practice court, simply practice the desired hitting motion in front of a mirror for five minutes a day. Learn how to time your shoulder turn away from the ball, then rotate into the shot and pull through, with your elbow extending and your wrist snapping at ball contact. It will take time for this overall motion to become second nature, but that's what you're striving for. I also think it's important for you to see this motion in the mirror to help convince you that you are capable of having a full, solid backhand swing.

Next, as you play, you need to remember that you don't have to kill the ball to be effective. Knowing your actual low-zone area (which you can determine by following the instructions on TK) should open you up to more offensive hitting, but if you presently have little confidence in your backhand, it will obviously take time and patience to make the change. In practice matches, develop a more aggressive approach by popping the ball at every reasonable opportunity, even though you may skip or leave up one shot after another. Greater power is what you're striving for, to go with your new outlook on the stroke, so swing through the ball and don't back off.

In time, your low-zone range and accuracy will improve and a new dimension will be added to your backhand, allowing you to become an offensive threat from that side.

Making Changes in Technique

While it's tempting to think we can simply *play* our way to better racquetball technique, the body is not that obliging. Any effort to train or retrain it to respond in a particular way takes time, patience, and persistence—not only in practice matches, but on an empty court and even in front of a mirror. Along the way you must weather frustrating periods of physical change, but if you pay your dues, the changes you seek will eventually give you a greater ability to score tough points as well as the easy points.

Following are some of the important steps that should be taken to acquire greater power, consistency, and versatility in your strokes.

RECOGNIZE THE NEED FOR BETTER TECHNIQUE

When you completely understand strategy, you know the value of being able to hit a particular shot, and this should motivate you to improve your execution. I find that when my students understand *why* they need to have a better stroke, they have greater patience trying to incorporate the necessary changes.

For example, if your toughest opponents are continually volleying in center-court rallies, but you lack this skill, a better understanding of low-zone racquetball will have you thinking, "I've never cut the ball off, but I can now see the value of scoring a lot of easy points this way." So this leads you to work on a better volleying-type stroke.

In a similar vein, let's say that you've always hit defensively from deep court but that you've stayed competitive with an excellent ceiling-ball game. Yet you also realize that the players you're trying to catch on the challenge ladder are all hitting good low-zone shots from back court and really putting pressure on their opponents. So if you're serious about your game, then it's time to go to work on the deficiencies you find in your technique.

UTILIZE VIDEO

I discussed in the Introduction why you should try to take advantage of videotape cameras and recorders, for this is the only way you can slow the game down enough to actually see the flaws in your strokes as you move to the ball and through impact. Using the checkpoints in this chapter, you can use slow-motion replays to provide an objective understanding of just how well you are swinging.

Videotape analysis is an indispensable learning tool, for there is often a huge difference between what you *think* you're doing as you swing and what you actually see yourself doing on the screen. I know that videotaping helps make me a more effective instructor. For instance, if I tell a student his racquet isn't high enough on the forehand setup, but he thinks it is, we have a serious communication problem. Yet when he sees himself on tape, he'll admit, "I can't believe the racquet is that low." Then we're on common ground and he's better motivated to make this necessary change in his swing.

Video also helps you recognize the exact moment when you have wasted motion in your swing. For the first time, you may realize that you have certain ingrained habits that you repeat and repeat without even knowing it—like touching your non-hitting hand to the racquet handle on your forehand.

If possible, try to have your strokes taped alongside an instructor or a top player at your club so that you have a role model and a point of reference when you study the tape.

TRY TO ELIMINATE THE "NUISANCE" MOVEMENTS

Not everybody has to swing the same to play this game well, but there are idiosyncrasies that very likely are detracting from your hitting efficiency. So as you strive to master a fundamentally sound stroke off both sides, streamline your motion as much as possible by eliminating—or at least minimizing—the unnecessary movements that cause inefficiency and narrow your margin of error, especially in center-court action.

Let's say, for example, that after studying yourself on videotape, you notice that your non-hitting hand is touching the racquet before you set up on the forehand, and that your non-hitting arm is staying in front of your body and interfering with your swing instead of pulling around to the side. You may still hit good shots, but you could hit *better* shots—easier and with more time—by eliminating these habits.

What you must do is mentally retrain your non-hitting hand and arm every time you hit, and this takes total concentration. If you work on the problem in practice, but don't really *think* about it as you play a match, then you will simply keep reverting back to your old habit. Instead, you must continually say to yourself, "I'm going to keep my arm out of the way," and think about nothing except that arm as you hit your forehand. Your body will rebel, but it can be retrained if you have the patience to fight through the transition period and not succumb to frustration when you don't see instant results.

Mastering good technique is an ongoing challenge, and you may need to spend a month or two trying to eliminate or incorporate small, subtle changes. But always keep in mind the fact that up the road, after a lot of practice and hard work, these bits and pieces will start soaking in and blending together. Then suddenly you'll realize that you've lifted your game to a higher level and upgraded your play to a point where you are beating some opponents who used to beat you.

LEARN TO BE YOUR OWN COACH

One of my important goals in this book has been to motivate you to spend time thinking about your game, analyzing it, and comparing it to the advice you are gathering here. Ideally, you'll try to become your own coach. Instructors and other players can provide advice, and video can reveal your errors on screen, but in the end you must get on an empty court and "coach" yourself to more effective strokes. Try to get a clear picture of your short-comings, whether they call for a major overhaul or subtle refine-ments, and then experiment with the concepts in this chapter and elsewhere in the book. Learn to recognize what actually works for you and what makes sense.

Here's an approach you might take to improve a particular stroke. Let's say that you're a strong player but your backhand is relatively ineffective; you swing too much with your arm and you roll your wrist over the ball in the hitting zone—and the result is simply too many skips. You've learned to live with this stroke, camouflaging the problem with an aggressive approach, but now that you recognize its limitations, ask yourself: "Am I willing to spend the time necessary to master a better stroke, where I get my body into the shot and the racquet comes through flat so I don't hit everything in the floor?"

If you have the determination to improve, making changes in your stroke should include five or ten minutes a day in front of a mirror, just swinging as I mentioned earlier. You simply want to work on the desired motion, getting a feel for the different new movements while checking yourself against the mirror at key points.

Next, you must get on an empty court and just bounce the ball, hitting one easy shot after another so that you grow more familiar with the desired motion and you're not worried or distracted by playing points. Standing and hitting like this may seem a bit boring, but this is the only way to acquire a solid, consistent motion that will hold up when you're competing. And if you're patiently persistent, the excitement will build as the changes eventually start to take hold. Many players, unfortunately, will make a conscientious effort in the beginning, but revert back to their old, limiting habits if they don't see some quick results.

Ideally, as you work on your stroking technique, strive for a sound motion that will continue to work well in the face of growing pressure and fatigue in a match you want to win. Once you have this basic swing "down," then you can learn to swing harder through that correct motion, and you can work on your ability to hit effectively while on the run, or while off-balance. Meanwhile, continue to be open to new subtleties that can bring further improvement.

As part of your ongoing self-coaching effort, emulating a player at your club can prove helpful—providing you're careful about just what you're trying to emulate. If, for example, you admire the way a person rips his backhand and you notice that he has a high setup with the wrist curled back, you may think that *that's* the key to his fantastic backhand. In reality, the reason this pro-style setup works is that he uses his body properly by rotating back and then driving through with shoulder and hip rotation. He also has exact timing in this difficult wrist snap. Another potential pitfall can arise if you work with an instructor who hasn't properly studied the game through videotape analysis and charting. Finding a competent instructor can be difficult, for there are relatively few qualified instructors around, and many instructors are conveying false information and flawed concepts about strategy and technique. This incorrect advice may not hurt a player right away, but if he continues to follow this advice for a year or two, his game will be plagued with shaky, ingrained habits that are tough to break just at the point when he wants to get his act together.

One way to increase the odds that you will find a qualified instructor is to call around your area to see who gets recommended the most. Then when you do sign up with an instructor you feel you can trust, be aware that he may explain the strokes differently than I do, since we all have our individual teaching approaches. Just remember that the top players all use the same stroking motion as they come through the hitting zone, and that's what you're striving to emulate. So make sure your instructor covers the major elements of the swing—setup, body movement into the shot, elbow bend and extension, wrist snap, and a sensible follow-through—while trying to eliminate unnecessary "extras." Aside from these overall stroking patterns, he should allow you to swing in a natural flow that fits your body build and athletic ability.

Some Closing Thoughts About the "Power" Game

In racquetball's "control era," before it became important to hit the ball with considerable power, swings were shorter in nature, with a high premium on accuracy. The forehand setup position had the elbow *below* the shoulder, and the swing was more compact, but it could still generate good power. On the backhand setup, the hitter's shoulders were basically parallel to the side wall, and the racquet wasn't drawn as far back or nearly as high as it is today. The result was an even-paced swing that produced a respectable offensive pace and considerable accuracy.

Since racquetball games all ran to 21 then, and no real blaster or shooter could outduel the top control players, most newcomers placed their emphasis on control instead of power. Then came Marty Hogan, who was the first to successfully challenge the "control group" that was perched at the top of the sport. He went through three or four years of learning to tame his blistering power, but when he gained control—in 1977—he became the unquestioned king of the hill.

I should note, however, that Marty was an unbelievably gifted athlete, with a rare ability to retain control at tremendously high velocity. Many other players in the years since have tried and failed to duplicate his feats by using his methods.

What Marty did do for the sport, though, was to make racquetball players stand up and take notice of the many virtues of hitting the ball harder. Increased pace on the ball significantly reduces an opponent's reaction time, as long as the ball is hit accurately. Simply put, power combined with control is much more dangerous to play against than just control.

Unfortunately, the quest for greater power led to considerable changes in swing emphasis: a much higher forehand setup (the elbow way above the shoulder) and shoulders facing the back wall on the backhand setup. Many players became enamored with a looping-type swing, where near-perfect timing was necessary— and tough to accomplish hit after hit.

The increased power in racquetball has brought considerable success to those players who know how to implement it, but it has caused widespread grief among the many players who either lack the necessary ability or common sense to use it intelligently. This is especially true at the club level, where many general C, B, and A players have taken the power theory to an unreasonable extreme. They try to duplicate these high, looping-type swings when they lack the physical ability to implement these strokes properly and consistently. Some of these players are impressive at times, maintaining their power over stretches of games and matches, but they can't maintain the necessary efficiency over a long haul.

So as you build and refine your game in the coming months and years, keep in mind that power *and* control are both integral parts of this game.

9

Drills to Improve Your Game

●

Since virtually every racquetball shot can be practiced alone or with a partner, it's easy for a racquetball player to improve his game. Playing by yourself, you can use the whole court as a practice machine, creating all the angles off the front wall, side wall, back wall, and ceiling. Meanwhile, it's incredible what two players can accomplish when they drill for 30 minutes every week instead of simply rushing into match-play competition, where their bottom-line concern is winning and losing.

This chapter will focus on eight favorite drills that I've designed for myself and for the people who come to my camps. These drills will challenge and improve your various rallying skills beyond the serve and serve return, whether you're on your own or with a rare—and treasured—partner who likes to drill, not simply hit-hit-hit and then start playing points.

By being creative with these and other drills in the book, you can prime yourself for a match or structure a workout that simulates almost an entire match. For example, if you have 10 or 15 minutes available on an empty court before you play, put yourself through a serving drill, the return drill (page TK), the 30-second drill using the front and side walls, a ceiling-ball exchange where you bring a few in long and a couple in short, the "rally right" and "rally left" drills, and a pinch-shot drill. Keep the movement going and you'll break into a good sweat and experience virtually all the shots in your upcoming match.

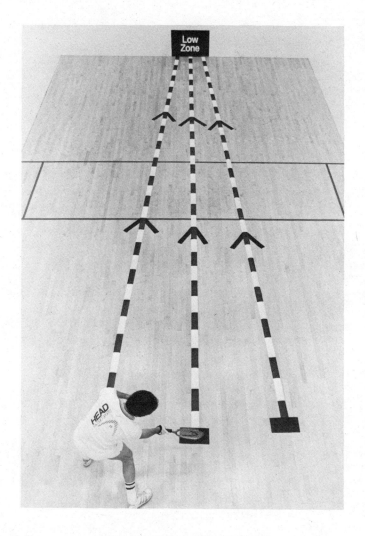

DRILL #1: THE 30-SECOND DRILL

The idea here is to simply rally by yourself with low-zone shots hit straight into the front wall. This may sound easy—until you try to keep this drill going for 30 seconds. Then you may realize that you have less control of your shots than you thought you did. By using the drill as often as possible, you will improve your ball control and racquet skills, enabling you to better capitalize on scoring opportunities in center-court. Start the drill 30 to 35 feet from the front wall.

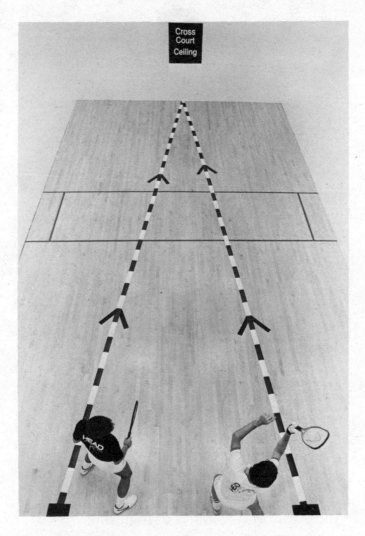

DRILL #2: THE TWO-PERSON CEILING-BALL DRILL

One person starts this drill by "serving" a ceiling ball to his opponent from deep court. The returner must go back to the ceiling, no matter how the initial ceiling shot was hit. After these first 2 ceiling balls, both players should consider themselves in a ceiling-ball rally and play it out accordingly, with each person looking for an offensive opportunity.

DRILL #3: THE INDIVIDUAL CEILING-BALL DRILL

Practice bringing in 3, 4, or 5 good ceiling balls (you pick the number), and then start looking for slight misses that you can pull into your low zone. After taking the shot, immediately move up to cover if you've left it up and attempt to score. This is excellent practice for making the transition from a high-zone rally to low-zone action.

Down
the Line

DRILL #4: RALLY RIGHT, RALLY LEFT

In photo 1, the player in the deep right corner tries to hit a passing shot down the right wall to force his opponent to the back right corner and out of center-court. The opponent in center-court tries to hold his ground (photo 2), cutting the ball off and driving it back down the right wall, hoping to keep his opponent in back court. The goal of this drill, which should be played on both the forehand and backhand sides, is to try to

maintain center-court control by hitting down-the-wall passing shots. Cross-court shots and pinches are not allowed.

During this drill, players will be continually exchanging and rotating positions, and should get out of each other's way so the drill can run smoothly.

DRILL #5: THE SLIDE-YOUR-BODY DRILL

This center-court drill shows how a player can learn to use his body legally to force his opponent off to the side during a rally. This smart body maneuvering opens up wide hitting lanes. Photos 1 through 3 show the

drill; notice how the player drops the ball over the hitting box (the black rectangle on the floor) and then slides to an open-stance hitting position in order to score down the open lane. Photo 4 shows how effectively this technique works against an opponent.

DRILL #6: THE DIAGONAL TOSS DRILL

This drill will extend your offensive capabilities whether you practice it alone or with a partner. When tossing the ball to a friend, use an underhand motion (photo 1), and try to make him stretch to his maximum coverage point (photo 2). When you're by yourself (photos 3, 4, 5), first learn to be comfortable hitting offensively as you move back. Then toss the ball so that you're forced to stretch as far as possible while still hitting offensively. Players who practice this drill learn to move back diagonally against cross-court passes and realize they can be offensive from deep court—even while hitting off-balance.

DRILL #7: THE DEEP CROSS-COURT RALLY

The two-person cross-court drill, in which players exchange cross-court passing shots, is excellent for learning the passing angles that can get the ball by your opponent. It's a strenuous drill because of the hard hitting involved from deep court, so rest every four or five minutes, and switch positions so that you learn the angles on both sides. Both players should maintain their positions at about 33 to 37 feet from the front wall.

DRILL #8: COVERING A SHOT HIT INTO THE BACK WALL

When your opponent drives the ball into the back wall, either by choice or in desperation, you must be able to fly-kill the shot after it rebounds off the front wall. As a two-person drill, the player behind drives the ball into the back wall (photo 1). Seeing this, the front player immediately moves up around the service zone and fly-kills the shot (photo 2). When you're practicing alone, pound the ball into the back wall from about 27 feet, then turn and hustle up to fly-kill the ball in front court.